Carpe Diem

The Ongoing Journey of an East Prussian Exile

Anneli Jones

Carpe Diem
The Ongoing Journey of an East Prussian Exile

by Anneli Jones
edited by Adam and Ben Jones

Published by Ōzaru Books, an imprint of BJ Translations Ltd
Street Acre, Shuart Lane, St Nicholas-at-Wade, BIRCHINGTON, CT7 0NG, UK
www.ozaru.net

First edition published 8 May 2023

ISBN: 978-0-9931587-3-5

Contents

List of photographs

Preface

Carpe Diem, 'seize the day' – indeed. If only we had learnt from Anneli how to do this, this book would have been better. Large parts of the text were in place even before *Reflections in an Oval Mirror* was published in 2008, ending with the fateful words "Vitya would decide where we should live", but we got bogged down in editorial discussions and actual editing, with the result that a full written account of her post-war life and visits back to East Prussia, in her own words, was not completed before her health started deteriorating, and she eventually died in 2011.

For over a decade since, we have been struggling to deal with the huge amount of material available to us: many hours of audio (reel to reel, cassette tapes), video (cine film, 8 mm and digital formats), several thousand photographs (over twenty albums, most with handwritten notes, and hundreds of negatives as well as numerous maps & diagrams), and hundreds of letters covering over six decades. Add to this the ever-increasing volume of material available online, in public (and private) archives, blogs, and of course books by other authors. The written materials alone come in English, German, French and Russian, in various scripts each needing to be deciphered through careful cross-referencing.

„Schluss, jetzt!" she might have said: "Stop here!". One has to call a halt sometime, and the centenary of her birth seems an apposite time to produce *something*, even if more can come later. Indeed, several friends who had been looking forward to discovering what happened to the various characters and places described in Reflections have sadly died in the interim, so we need to draw a line and publish now for those who are still with us.

In one sense, she intended *Carpe Diem* to refer only to the immediate post-war period, when she boldly accepted the hand that fate had dealt her. It had been her motto since a young age, but increasingly served to guide her through the turmoil of war, and of love and loss. However, this attitude of 'if Fate sends you lemons, start a lemonade-stand' also pervaded her adult activities, which are equally deserving of being remembered – albeit in a limited form initially.

The book is therefore imperfect, yet we hope it is still interesting, perhaps even inspiring. It's tempting to label it "Volume 1 of ___ " but given past experience, we should make no promises about further publication of related material in future. Yet the hope – and the materials – are there. All we need to do is *Carpe Diem*.

Adam Jones, Ben Jones

8 May 2023
Anneli's 100th birthday

Vergebens, dass Ihr ringsum wissenschaftlich schweift,
Ein jeder lernt nur, was er lernen kann;
Doch der den Augenblick ergreift,
Das ist der rechte Mann.
Ihr seid noch ziemlich wohl gebaut,
An Kühnheit wird's Euch auch nicht fehlen,
Und wenn Ihr Euch nur selbst vertraut,
Vertrauen Euch die andern Seelen.

'tis in vain through 'knowledge' that you stray,
Each one learns only what he can;
But they that boldly seize the day...
Now there's the measure of a man!
Well-built you are, and fearless too:
Trust yourself! They'll trust in you.

Goethe (Faust I:4)

Refugee Memories

When we crossed the River Elbe at Dannenberg in March 1945, we knew that we had reached the point of no return. I realized that up to that moment, for nearly five months on an open wagon, I had cherished a secret hope of returning to the old life at home in East Prussia, but this was a demarcation line.

West of the Elbe we were no longer treated as migrants, passing through towns and villages, receiving daily helpings of swede soup, but as refugees requiring a semi-permanent home.

We were told to go towards Uelzen, then to proceed north towards Bremervörde, but my mother refused: "We are not far from Celle, where my son is being trained as a soldier, and that is where we are going first," Mutti said in a very firm tone which the officials had to obey. So southwards we travelled. All of us, including our horses, were very hungry and tired when we stopped near a village on the outskirts of Celle. Mutti went by tram to the centre of Celle. I would have loved to go with her to see my brother, but felt obliged to remain with the others, to beg or steal food for the animals and for us. At that moment even the much-disliked swedes boiled in water would have been welcome. We picked clover and grass, wiped it as clean as we could, then ate it as a salad. Meanwhile Mutti was given a real meal by the friends to whom we had sent some of our precious possessions at a time when such panic action was strictly forbidden in East Prussia. I remembered my sister Marlene packing that "gift parcel", as we called it to disguise the real purpose. She and our cousin Jutta had giggled at the idea of tricking officialdom. Now Mutti was going to retrieve that particular package.

It was growing dark by the time my mother came back to us, accompanied by a man who looked only vaguely familiar to me. He was carrying our parcel, the gift wrapping still intact. It was too dark to see Mutti's eyes, but I could tell by the tone of her voice that she had been crying: my brother Claus had not been in the barracks. He had been sent into battle before his training was finished. So he might yet be killed in the last days or months of the war, as Mutti's younger brother had been killed in 1918. The worry of what might happen seemed worse than the knowledge of his death would have been; but, like Mutti, I did not want the others to see me cry. So we all put on a brave face and joked about the stupid officials who had not even opened our parcel. It was hilarious, and our laughter reminded me of the film "Forget-me-not", where Gigli played a clown on the stage just after he had lost the person he had most loved. His song, "*Ride bajazzo*" (Laugh now, clown), had haunted me ever since.

The uncertainty about Claus affected me much more deeply than the discovery that my father, Väti, had died of starvation in a Russian camp. We had been through many months of uncertainty and vague hopes before another farmer from the Darkehmen district gave us this information, and longer still until the Russian authorities sorted out their documents to confirm individual prisoner histories.

Berlin _ _ _ _ _ _ _ _ _ , den 3.August _ _ 19 49

D er Volkssturmmann, Landwirt Adolf Ernst

W i e m e r _ _ _ _ _ _ _ _ _ _ _ _ _ _ ,

wohnhaft in ~~Berlin~~ Mickelau, Kreis Angerapp/Ostpreußen,

_ ,

ist am 10.März 1945 _ _ _ um _ _ _ Uhr _ _ _ _ Minuten
zu unbekannter Stunde _ _ _ _ _ _ _ _ _ _ _ _
in ~~Berlin~~ Kowno im Lagerlazarett _ _ _ _ _ _ verstorben.

D er Verstorbene war geboren am 14.Dezember 1894 _ _ _

in Paupelken. _

(Standesamt _ _ _ _ _ _ _ _ _ _ _ _ _ _ _ Nr. _ _ _ _)

D er Verstorbene war ~~nicht~~ verheiratet mit Wanda Klara

Elise Wiemer geborenen Hahn. _ _ _ _ _ _ _ _ _

_ _ _ _ _ _ _ _ _ _ _ _ _ _ _ _ _ _ _ _

Eingetragen auf ~~mündliche~~ schriftliche — Anzeige _ _ _ _ _
der Deutschen Dienststelle für die Benachrichtigung der nächsten
Angehörigen von Gefallenen der ehemaligen deutschen Wehrmacht

Auf Grund eigener Ermittlungen wurden der Beruf

~~D Anzeigende~~ und ein Vorname des Verstorbenen

sowie zwei Vornamen der Ehefrau eingetragen.-

Eine Zwischenzeile. _ _ _ _ _ _ _ _ _ _ _ _ _

~~Vorgelesen, genehmigt und unterschrieben~~

_ _ _ _ _ _ _ _ _ _ _ _ _ _ _ _ _ _

Der Standesbeamte

In Vertretung: *Jäger*

Todesursache: Ruhr.

Väti's death certificate

Cause is "Typhus", in a camp hospital. Issued in August 1949 but first seen in January 2021.
The 'burial' record in Kaunas, Lithuania states "Adolf Wiemer was not recovered during our
re-interment activities. The planned transfer to the collective cemetery in Kaunas was,
therefore, unfortunately not possible. His name is recorded in a particular place."

Laughing and joking, we travelled through Lower Saxony without noticing the very different appearance of the houses. It was really dark by now, but we were determined to reach the end of our journey.

In the village of Weertzen we were directed on to a small road leading through a little forest and across a very small bridge into the hamlet called Freyersen. There the family of Farmer Brinkmann was expecting us; Farmer Heinz next door expected the Seefeldts "and two working men". As Farmer Brinkmann had expected only one working man, we decided that Little Volodya and Dyeda should go to the farm next door, while Big Volodya with Marusha and Verushka stayed with us. Katya became a maidservant with the Dittmer family further down the village road. She was later probably repatriated to her beloved Ukraine – keeping my fur jacket, which I had lent her during our trek.

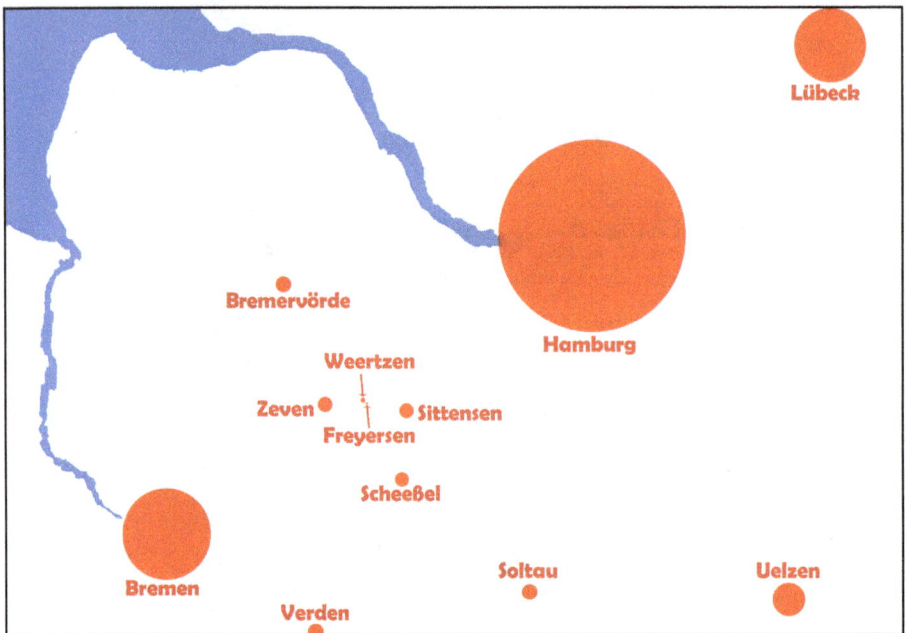

Map of Freyersen area

Our carriage was directed into a large barn-like building: a few milking cows lived in a box on our right, horses in various boxes on the left, where our horses were given a stand after they had pulled the carriage through the gable doors into the large empty space between the animal boxes. Next to the cows stood a pump and various facilities for washing milk-cans and people. From here a smaller door led outside towards pigsties, chicken-house and toilet. Near the horse boxes stood a ladder leading up to a hay and straw loft. We were led through a small door opposite the large entrance doors into an enormous farm kitchen.

There we saw a huge stove – even larger than our stove at home had been. Next to it a door led into the farmer's family compartments, and opposite this door was another leading to the daughter's room. Her name was Marianne and she, like two of her brothers, still went to school; the eldest brother Heini was already working on the farm and about to be married, we were told by Mimi, the stout and friendly farmer's wife. I never discovered where all these boys slept, except that the youngest, little Günter, had a bed in his parents' room. Maybe Heini and Hannes spent their nights with the Albers family, a rich farmer living in a grand house at the entrance to Freyersen. Frau Albers was Frau Brinkmann's sister. Herr Albers was a dried-up gentlemanly man; Herr Brinkmann was slim and lively and very interested in any subject from farming to politics and even art.

Between the two doors – leading to the family room and to Marianne's opposite – stood a long table under the windows looking out to the yard. This was the family's and sometimes our dining room table. On the wall hung a telephone, maybe the only phone in the little village, for which Herr Brinkmann held the licence for other people's use. He charged a fixed sum per call per minute, as the phone could only cope with outgoing local calls, that is to say as far as either Hamburg or Bremen. (Freyersen is situated roughly half-way between the two cities.) Maybe it was Frau rather than Herr Brinkmann who was in charge of the phone, as she was the more domineering of the two.

Another door from the kitchen led into the "Gästediele" which sounds very grand[1] considering that it was to become our refugee entrance for the next few years. From this large entrance hall one door led to the little room where there was hardly any space except for the huge double bed for the Golubov family. Marusha settled on this to feed baby Verushka and put her to sleep, while Big Volodya came to look at our room opposite theirs: we had a big double bed in the left corner, a plush-covered sofa along the adjoining wall, several chairs, a stove for heating and cooking in one corner and one fairly large window looking out to the front entrance, to the Heinz's farm and to an outside bread-baking oven between the two farms. Vitya could easily run across from his father's and grandfather's room to ours, but he gradually came to accept our room as his. He slept in our big bed between Mutti and me, which was similar to Vitya's place between Dyeda and his son Little Volodya in the Heinz's farmhouse.

We settled in fairly easily. Together with the Golubovs we shared a wardrobe standing in the entrance hall. A cupboard for the farmer's preserves was in the same hall, which was cool, because all walls faced north. In summer a little sunlight reached us in the evening, and Vitya often played by our front door. I frequently sat next to him, stitching new clothes out of old items. A red-and-white chequered dirndl dress made out of maids' bed linen turned out quite successful and, in a way, so did a dress I made out of two satin dresses of my mother's. I cut these into long strips and stitched them together lengthways, using the vertical strips for the skirt part, horizontal strips for body and sleeves. I was so proud of my hand-stitched masterpiece that I decided to save it in the wardrobe for special occasions; but, alas, when such an occasion arose I found large holes in my special dress and a mouse's nest at the bottom of the wardrobe. Mice were the curse of our new home; the house had no damp course, so it had to be ventilated by long openings to the outside, an open-door invitation to mice.

---

[1] Literally "Guests' Hallway"

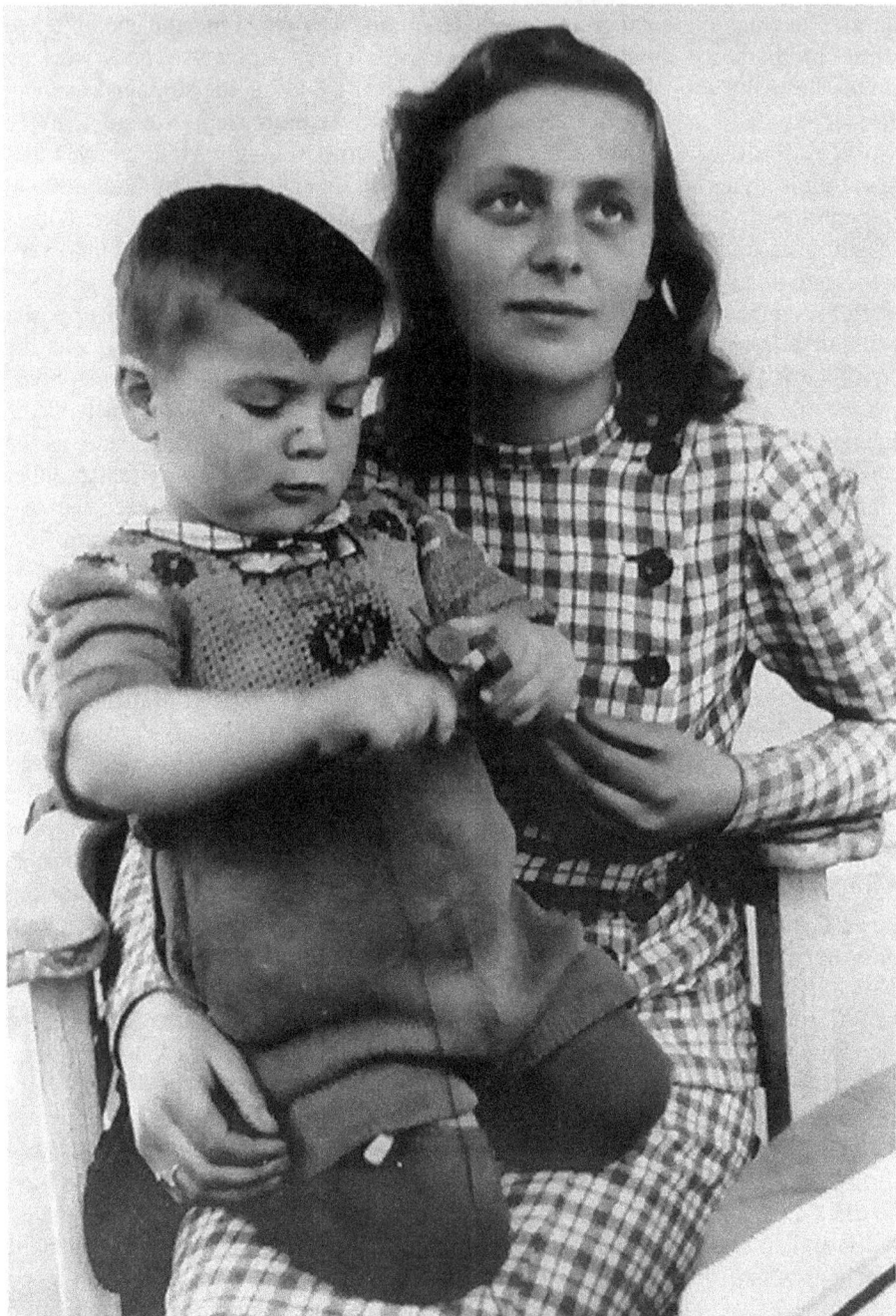

Vitya and Anneli

So I gave up sewing and joined Mutti in her efforts to do fieldwork, which I enjoyed rather more than she did. But she persevered, just as she persevered with new skills such as peeling potatoes. Watching her struggle was hilarious, and she happily joined in my laughter. Actually I was not much better myself.

As we did not live far from Hamburg I decided to visit my Labour Service friend Rita Eggers. There was a narrow-gauge station in Weertzen, less than half a mile from Freyersen. Trains ran quite frequently to Tosted, where one could join the main line to Hamburg-Harburg. So, while Mutti was planning the best way to travel to Schwarzenberg to fetch Marlene, I set off with Vitya. The little boy was impressed by the huge crowds of people, especially at Harburg station, where we got out. "*Soo viele Mänschen!*" he shouted in his broad East Prussian accent. "Look at the little East Prussian boy," I heard several people remark, and I was proud of Vitya's linguistic achievements.

Most of the air raid damage was in Hamburg proper, but Harburg was close enough to suffer. Rita's father, a homoeopath, charged his patients in terms of food rather than money and so the Eggers family were better off than most people in wartime Germany. It was a long time since I had had a grand meal such as Rita's mother produced. Her father was so impressed with Vitya, he could not stop photographing him, especially after Rita herself had showered us with lovely items of clothing, mainly old, but perfect dresses of hers for me.

Rita told me of her new boyfriend, a Brazilian student called Vamir. If they did decide to marry, Rita would happily move to Brazil. Vitya and I wanted to go back to Freyersen that night, so we never had time to meet Vamir.

Mutti was in a hurry to set out for Marlene because war was nearing its end and she wanted to be back with me by then. I told her that I was quite sure that the war would not end before my birthday. "Nevertheless, British or American troops might come earlier," she said. But before the British army arrived, we had another frightening visitor: Rita appeared one morning with her boyfriend. They had walked all the 50-60 miles from Hamburg, sleeping in odd sheds or under bushes during the day. Why? Because Brazil had entered the war on the side of the Western Powers, and now Himmler had become *Gauleiter* of Hamburg and had begun to arrest all enemy-related foreign students.

Of course we agreed to put them up, but had no clear idea where and moreover, how to justify Vamir's presence. The space problem was solved relatively easily: there was room on our floor and all we had to do was to send Vamir into the hall while we undressed. The justification for his arrival was rather trickier. We decided to make him our long-lost Argentinian cousin whose name was Vamir Hahn. "Any stranger staying here for more than three days has to register with the Bürgermeister", Mimi informed us. "Of course," I said while my legs began to shake. Already the local shopkeeper's mother, an ardent Nazi woman who was rumoured to kneel and pray in front of Hitler's portrait, had apparently reported my relationship with "a Russian child" to the Nazi party office in Zeven, already I was quite scared, and now the added Vamir problem! I was scared, even more so when Mimi Brinkmann offered to take Vamir in her farm wagon. "No, thank you," I said politely, "it is a nice walk through the heath and we shall all enjoy it." And so we did, looking over our shoulders to see if anyone was watching. Nobody seemed to be there. So we sat on the still wintry carpet of heather behind a gorse bush while Rita alone slowly walked to the village to register, later proudly showing us the stamp in her passport. We all dawdled back home and told the worried Brinkmanns that it had been done. Rita even showed them her stamped document.

Allied Officers

Everything had gone well. In April, Mutti had managed to bring Marlene despite an air raid on Hanover station. But never in my life had I prayed as ardently as I now prayed for the arrival of the Allied troops. God must have heard me, I thought; for there they were, three days later, the British army with a few Dutchmen in their ranks. They turned us out of the houses to make room for their soldiers: the Brinkmann family went to their Albers relatives, we were sent to the Dittmers' chicken-house. Vamir introduced himself as an ally and was given permission to stay in our room with his girlfriend. He did not turn an eyelid to help us, and if I had not looked forward to the chicken-house, I would have been furious. Instead I offered Rita the use of my accordion and at night we heard their musical parties ringing from "our" room downhill.

Volodya, Dyeda and Vitya also joined us in the chicken-house. We cleaned up the drop trays, put some blankets on them and then we could sleep, Mutti, Marlene and I with heads to one end, Volodya with his father and son to the other end. Some of our longer legs were slightly overlapping. Before we went to sleep, we cooked on an open fire outside and chatted to our occasional visitors.

Life in the chicken-house gave me a new perspective inasmuch as I recognized visitors by their legs. I found some cheerful material to sew curtains for the small windows at floor level. Jars with some early spring flowers made our room look pretty. So we were not ashamed to receive the odd member of the British army as our guest. They were all generous guests, bringing rare luxuries like chocolate for Vitya, sometimes coffee or tea for us. One nice Dutch sergeant – or maybe he was an officer? I could not tell the signs of different ranks – was extremely indignant that I of all people, who had taken care of a little Russian child, should live in such conditions while Rita and Vamir lived in relative luxury. He wanted to put in an official complaint, but I protested that the whole point of my care for Vitya was my belief that there should not be a distinction between people of different nationalities and so I could not accept to be singled out among others. He did not agree, but consented to do nothing but write a letter of recommendation for me to get an interpreter's job with military government. I really laughed at the thought of myself interpreting with my few words of school English, but he persuaded me to give it a try, because the military authorities were very short of people with a clean political record who could speak German. I agreed to try. The occupation army left our village, Vamir went with them and we moved back into the Brinkmanns' house, which we found in surprisingly good order. Rita said that she had looked after the place.

8 May 1945

Then came my birthday, 8 May, and still no sign of the peace I had expected to come that day, still those battle noises all around us. We had heard that Hitler had committed suicide about a week earlier, though I found that hard to believe. But as it was a beautiful sunny day, Rita and I decided to walk to Zeven to take my Dutchman's letter to the military governor. Rita's English was actually better than mine, but she did not want to try for the job, because she hoped to be able to return to Harburg soon.

I felt my heart beating under my chin when I sat in the governor's waiting room. I did not have to wait long before I was called in and politely offered a chair opposite the desk. When I looked into the kindest deep blue eyes I had ever seen, all my fears evaporated and I regained a sense of humour regarding my interpreter's skills. Capt. Morrison, the deputy governor of the Canadian Military Government, within the British Zone covering the Ruhr, spoke no German at all and thus experienced the full extent of my ignorance of the English language. Nevertheless he wanted to know the address where he could pick me up the next morning and on future mornings until he had managed to rent me a room in Zeven. I could have danced for joy and wanted to skip all the way back to Freyersen, but it was too hot and we both soon grew tired. Elation does not carry legs for long.

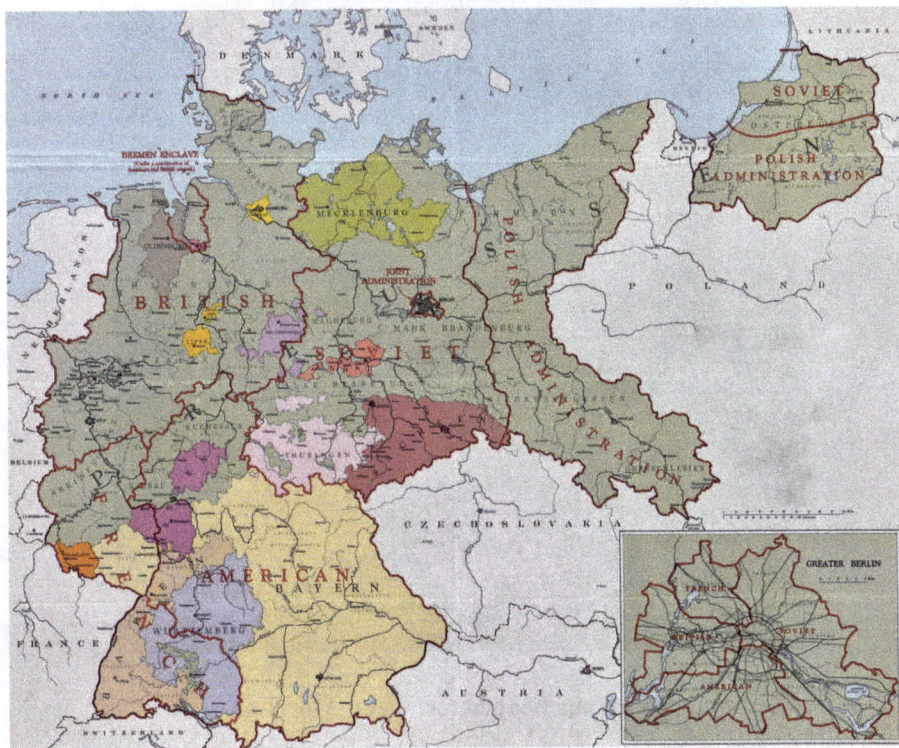

The division of Germany

Rita heard the noise of an engine behind us. "What is the best way of hiking a lift, to look perkily attractive or totally worn out?" Rita asked. We did not have time to decide, just lifted our thumbs. It worked. One of the two British soldiers came to sit in the back of the van with us and interrogated us. He reassured me that a German surrender was imminent this same day, so I had been right to hope for such an important birthday present.

The two soldiers had been to Lübeck to explore the feasibility of arranging a newspaper office and printing press and were going back to Bad Godesberg near Bonn, where they were presently printing an army paper. As I had told him I had originally intended to become a journalist, he said he would fetch me to their new offices as soon as possible. One of these rash, casual promises that people make, I thought. Nevertheless, just to be on the safe side, I told him I would not consider the job unless my student friend Edith, who now lived near Bad Godesberg, could also come. He seemed to agree, perhaps because I told him that Edith was a very beautiful girl.

With our benefactor, Capt. Morrison

12

In order not to prevent them from entering the motorway at Sittensen, I said that we could be put down in Weertzen and walk that little stretch to Freyersen, but the soldier insisted on taking us right to our house. Vitya came running towards me with outstretched arms, calling "Mama, Mama!" I explained to the soldier that Vitya was not my biological child, but a Russian half-orphan. That really impressed the man, who introduced himself as Tristan Jones. He was a communist and therefore loved all things Russian, he said. I thought, what a stupid way to look at things, but I was still staring at him with an open mouth, the first real communist I had ever met. Mutti offered the men coffee and biscuits which she had managed to acquire from some Hamburg evacuees living across the road. She was very impressed with this Mr Jones who spoke such good German, and they had an animated conversation until it was time for the two men to leave. Later that evening we heard that the war had really ended and saw the spectacle of the German army blowing up its last ammunition like fireworks. Most of us danced for joy; some were subdued, wondering what the future might hold.

Next morning Capt. Morrison came to fetch me in a very comfortable car. I introduced him to Mutti, Marlene and Vitya; even Mimi wanted to be seen to meet that kind Canadian captain. Then we were off. Our conversation was quite ridiculous with my peculiar English. At one point I searched for the word 'tree' and eventually described it as "one of those long things that stand in woods with leaves on the top." Fancy remembering all those words and not the simple word 'tree'! Similar incidents happened frequently, but I gradually learnt English.

On this first working day we visited the mayor of Zeven, who most probably had been a Nazi, but was such a kind and gentle man that it was impossible to attach any kind of politics to him. He genuinely felt himself to be Morrison's friend and called him his benefactor. So did Mutti when one day a load of furniture, crockery, cutlery and other household items arrived from a former Labour Service camp near Zeven. Mutti kept some of the armchairs and the round table until she died, and I still have the ivory, gold-rimmed soup cups. The cutlery with the RAD engravings was probably too embarrassing to keep for long. Capt. Morrison took me to a shop to buy dress materials and found a dressmaker in Zeven to sew them.

I was embarrassed about such gestures, though they were like nothing compared with the riches Mayor Kennedy, the governor, heaped on his interpreters – or should I say mistresses? I was introduced to the Bremervörde crowd on my third day of work and I especially liked the beautiful actress from Hamburg who had no inhibitions about her love for sex and beautiful clothes. A Dutch girl called Peggy was also very nice. I did not like the Czech-born former hairdresser at all. She was married to a German who had not yet come back from the war, or, if he had, was not seen anywhere near his wife. She exploited Kennedy's largesse to the full: he bought her a large hairdresser's saloon and equipped it with all the latest professional furniture, specially ordered from Hamburg. On another floor of her saloon was her private flat with ultra-modern furniture, an always full drink cabinet with ridiculous bar seats and Venetian blinds on all the large windows. Kennedy rented a maid for his mistress, and she served at grand dinners for four, dressed in black with a white cap and apron. Candles gleaming on the silver embellished the atmosphere. The "Czech" lady was obviously buying a future from the mayor.

Outside the town she acquired a hunting lodge where she spent weekends with her lover. Surprisingly, with all her lovemaking, the actress was not at all jealous.

And then there was the attractive, dramatic Russian interpreter Vera, whose stares of animosity towards me I found at times unbearably sad. At odd occasions she relented, such as when Volodya invited us to his birthday party at the Heinz's farm. He had set out a beautiful table, albeit with cheap glasses that he could break with impunity. The meal consisted of potatoes, cabbage and masses of fat pork. They served some genuine vodka as well as home-made drinks. (It was against the law to distil drinks, yet many country people did it.) There was much singing – Vera had a beautiful voice – toasting, breaking of glasses and a great deal of general noise. Vera was so tipsy that she became quite affectionate even towards me. Vera was radiant. She was at home in this atmosphere, I thought, and not with Capt. Laurie, whatever she imagined. Capt. Morrison also enjoyed himself. He asked Vera to sing "Black Eyes", the only Russian song he knew, and everybody joined in. I had never experienced so many eyes sparkling with such happiness as during this vodka party. Morrison's bright blue eyes and his cheerful, kind laughter almost made me cry. He did not drink as much as the rest of us who did not have to drive.

Herr Emde in the window of his chemist's shop

I tried to persuade him to spend the night in Mutti's room, but he declined the invitation. So I also chose to go back to Zeven with him, where he had meanwhile rented two rooms for me at the pharmacist Emde's family house. Letting rooms to the Military Government was a good defence against being obliged to let to large refugee families. One of my rooms was downstairs and had a grand piano in it. The other was a bright, modern bedroom upstairs with a view of the garden and Mrs Emde's numerous dogs of the Spitz breed. She had a grown-up son, but her real children were these white, long-haired dogs. Usually I was invited to have breakfast on the terrace, but I avoided dogs' playtime. In spite of these four or five little rascals the garden was in beautiful order.

Mr and Mrs Emde consumed great quantities of alcohol, some bought, the rest distilled in their pharmacy. He was a Freemason and often teased about it by his wife. They were both very kind. I was encouraged to have as many parties as I liked. Both of them loved parties – and so did the dogs. When some of the Zeven doctors came for drinks with the Emdes they relied on Morrison's kind heart to see them home after curfew.

I was upset to discover that the Emdes sold medicines for butter and eggs. I did not tell them what I thought about black marketeering.

A British doctor, Dr Henry Phin of No. 5 Field Dressing Station, had a reputation of being a real German-hater. I found this not to be true, he was kind and generous to Germans who suffered from some ailments. Some people obviously just assumed hatred because they knew he was a Jew. He told me that his home was in Morpeth, in the North of England and invited me to visit him there. But I never took his address.

I felt responsible for Dr Schaper's house which had been requisitioned for Morrison in Zeven, not for political reasons, but because it was a really good house. So we tried to save it from uninvited guests coming to Morrison's parties and drinking. Dr Phin was always welcome, and so was the officer who claimed to be related to Churchill[2]. He was very much a gentleman. He addressed me in a polite manner and found good stables and food for two of our riding horses in Zeven for a time.

A Polish lieutenant called Cziblowski, who had himself been in a concentration camp and had every reason to hate Germans, was one of the politest people at headquarters. He tried to build bridges between Vera and me (and to put the embarrassed Polish girl Lucy at ease) by repeatedly telling them about me and Vitya – which in turn made me feel embarrassed.

I don't remember how I came to join parties in a sergeants' mess at the Reichshof Hotel, which were more fun than Military Government parties. A nice Dutch sergeant called Bill was always singing "There are rats, rats, bigger than the cats..." or "Lilli Marlene". Usually we raided the pantry for midnight feasts, but one day they had lost the key. Sgt Visher took an axe to smash the door... but the axe-handle broke. "Made in Germany", he laughed. Eventually we broke the door. Some items which the sergeants called "awful army food" were delicacies for me: corned beef (they called it bully-beef), tinned pink salmon, dried apricots, peaches, baked beans.

Vitya

I saw Vitya several times a week. Sometimes he stayed with me overnight, sometimes I spent the night in Freyersen. So it was a great shock when Volodya told me that they would move into a large refugee camp about 25 km away. They

---

[2] See page 26

hoped for immigration papers to America or Australia, and that was why they had to take Vitya along to register his name. Volodya took me for a long walk in Freyersen, pleading with me to marry him and come with them. I needed time to think, but I really needed time to cry privately, in my bedroom. I liked Volodya well enough, even when he kissed me, but did I really have to choose between Vitya with his father and no Vitya at all? That night, quite unusually for me, I spent hours praying to God for guidance. Volodya agreed that once all the papers were arranged, he and Dyeda would travel ahead to have everything ready for Vitya, who could stay with me during that time. We could take him to Freyersen where he had his beloved heathland to play in, to make up his own games and wait for me to collect him for the night. But meanwhile Vitya would have to register and live in the camp for a time. Capt. Morrison would take me to the camp at least once a week. This seemed by no means enough for me, nor would it be for Vitya, who would feel deserted. I could not stop howling.

Capt. Morrison and I went to the camp after the Mosins had gone there for five days. Vitya came running into my arms and clung to me happily for a few minutes, then ran off to play with new friends. That much seemed satisfactory, but the condition of the camp itself seemed to leave much to be desired, both in terms of cleanliness and of cooking facilities. I just hoped they would not have to live there for long.

All these Nissen huts, several families squeezed into one, and all that babble of voices, especially near one hut, where a makeshift table provided for a double-wedding party. One of the radiant brides was Marusha! She was wearing a short lace curtain pinned to her hair with flowers. Big Volodya, the groom, looked at us a little sheepishly. "We could not tell you before that we were not married. You might have thought us immoral." And Marusha grinned happily: "Now you cannot take him away from me", thus explaining all her former hysterical scenes of jealousy.

Nicht in die ferne Zeit verliere dich!
Den Augenblick ergreife!
Der ist dein.

Do not lose yourself in time far off!
Seize the moment!
It is yours.

Schiller (Macbeth)

Repatriation

It was less than a week since our visit to the camp when we were woken in the chemist's shop in the middle of the night. Outside stood both our Russian families, calling on me to hide them quickly. We ushered them indoors and listened to their report in the dark. The British authorities had reluctantly acceded to Soviet pressure to repatriate their citizens, and so a commission had arrived at the camp. Our two families were really frightened, the Mosins did not at all cherish the prospect of returning to a village where all their family had been cruelly massacred by heaven knows whom; the Golubovs had a most real fear for their lives. Big Volodya now confessed what other Russians on the farm had long suspected, namely that he was a deserter from the Soviet army and that Marusha and later the German troops had helped him to escape. A return to his home would inevitably have meant a court martial for him and some other court for Marusha, who had assisted him. We had to talk in whispers in case someone had followed them. They must live in rooms without windows on to the street. Baby Verushka did not understand the necessity for whispering voices. None of us felt the slightest obligation to comply with a cruel agreement signed by the British; nor, as it turned out, did Capt. Morrison. With his help our Russian visitors could comfortably live in hiding until a new camp was established solely for prospective emigrants overseas to various nations on the other side of the world.

The new camp was a less crowded, healthier place, yet it seemed that the change had come too late for little Vitya. A very worried Volodya came towards our car when we arrived for a visit. Vitya had been taken to hospital three days earlier. "Why didn't you phone?" I asked.

"There was no point. He has scarlet fever and one can only look at him through the small window of the isolation ward."

We drove Volodya from the camp to the hospital, a distance of 10 km which he had walked every day. He then took us to a window where we could peer into a gloomy room. I could not make out who among those wretched little figures was Vitya. Volodya decided that he was not there any more. So we went to look for the ward sister, to whom I explained that I was the mother of Victor Mosin.

She raised her hands in horror: "Oh my God! We did not know! If we had known that he had a German mother…" – her voice petered out.

"I'm listening."

"Well, I mean there was nothing we could do. He caught diphtheria on top of scarlet fever, you see…"

"Are you trying to tell me that he died?"

She nodded with a frightened glance in Capt. Morrison's direction. Neither he nor Volodya had been able to follow the conversation. I could not bear the way Volodya looked at me, like a little dog pleading for a bone.

Suddenly I knew that it was all my fault, that I had neglected them. To be kind to him now… how? Anything I could do would be heaping insult on to injury.

Volodya understood the long silence. "Our Vitya, all finished?"

I nodded.

"Where is he?"

I looked to the ward sister for an answer to Volodya's question.

"No, you can't see him now. We must first tidy…" she stammered, "I mean disinfect," she added with a sigh.

I imagined Vitya's corpse dumped on a pile, in a way that a German mother and a Canadian officer would find objectionable and that would break Volodya's heart.

"So when can we come?" I asked.

"Tomorrow morning."

I told Volodya about the need for disinfection and said that we could come next morning. But I felt he knew, or suspected what was also in my mind. He smiled a little when he replied: "Not we, only I. You good Mama for live Vitya, me Papa for all my dead children."

I was such a coward, I did not insist on helping.

We drove back to the camp in silence. Only Capt. Morrison was crying openly. He told Volodya he would send a car to take him to hospital early next day and Volodya gratefully accepted the offer. He would let us know the funeral arrangements, he added in a matter-of-fact voice. But then he embraced me and we cried together.

Capt. Morrison left me with Mutti and Marlene that night.

On the day of the funeral Vitya looked happy lying among the heather which was just beginning to bloom. He had always loved heather and called a small patch of it in the Freyersen forest "my special place". Now he was wearing the blue and white striped sailor suit that had once belonged to Claus. His cheeks were red, and a light breeze moved streaks of his soft fair hair across his forehead. For a moment I thought it might tickle him and that he would open his eyes and stretch out his hands to stroke the heath he loved so much. But when it was my turn to kiss the cold hard face in the open coffin, I knew he was dead and that it no longer mattered when the lid was put over the body and the coffin disappeared into the hole below. All of us, Mutti, Marlene, even Capt. Morrison threw a handful of earth down to Vitya, now so far away from us.

Josyn   Viktor   3.9.45   jo   291/1945

All that officially remains of Vitya

Volodya had arranged a funeral feast at an inn, not far from the cemetery. The wake was a farewell party, and not only for Vitya. Volodya proposed a toast to me "who had been Vitya's good and loving mother for so long" and Dyeda said a simple "thank you" as he lifted his glass and looked at me. His open eyes had lost their kind sparkle and looked far more dead than Vitya's closed eyes. That much for "Boshe", the one who had preserved Vitya for something special. Would Dyeda ever pray again?

Before our winter began, the two men left for the summer in Australia. I never heard from them again, but had some news about them via Marusha, who went to the United States at the same time and later had another three children. Big Volodya worked on a mink fur farm in Wisconsin, where the young son of the owner had seen a photo of Marlene and had written to her. Volodya had probably hoped to do some match-making.

News of the family

We also had news of Claus via Armand Claussin, the Belgian prisoner-of-war who had with great foresight given everyone his home address. Marlene had not required it, as, miraculously, most of the many letters which Mutti wrote during our time on the road and optimistically popped into letterboxes whenever she saw one, had indeed reached her, and had given her a fairly true idea of our whereabouts. But thanks to this we learned that Claus was alive and as well as could be expected – he had been transferred from a Belgian POW camp to one in Scotland, where he was very happy.

Meanwhile Mutti received an eyewitness report of my father's death in a Russian camp in Lithuania. We had heard rumours before then, but the confirmation still hit us hard. I went to the toilet more often than before so that I could give way to my tears without others noticing them, and I believe Mutti did the same. But for the rest of the world, we were our usual, joking, happy selves.

We had also received news from Omi. Mutti began to sob uncontrollably when she came to the part of Annelore's letter which described how Omi had lost consciousness during the hard refugee trek. But the letter went on to say that she had recovered and was now living with her son Arnold and family in Schleswig-Holstein, hoping to join us whenever possible. Capt. Morrison volunteered to take us there to fetch Omi. Would she dare to go in this fast modern thing called a car? "We could take a sledge hammer to knock her out", I suggested. In the event it proved unnecessary. Onkel Arnold's place was far more beautiful than our room in Freyersen, a pretty bungalow on the shore of a lake with a landing stage and a sailing boat belonging to a Hamburg family who had first accommodated the Hahn family as refugees, but soon allowed Arnold to buy the property for a price fixed before the currency reform. He became a keen fisherman, catching enormous fish in the idyllic Blunker See. Tante Lena devoted her energy to the garden surrounding their house and sloping towards the lake. Onkel Arnold had bought extra land on top of the hill by the road leading down to their bungalow. He had built a cellar into the bank and was bubbling with plans, all in a very natural, non-mechanical way. I would have loved to live there, but Omi was most anxious to come and live with her daughter, just as her mother, my great-grandmother Omut, had come to live with her when both women were widows.

After Hamburg black-market coffee and Tante Lena's wonderful gateaux we departed with Omi in the car.

More Allied Officers

Without Vitya or me – not to speak of Rita and Vamir – the Freyersen room seemed quite spacious enough to accommodate Omi. After a very careful, gentle drive by Capt. Morrison, Omi was happy to see her new home.

Morrison and I continued with our daily tasks which he had explained to me in these words: "Our job is to get rid of Nazis as quickly as possible without leaving too many gaps in the administration of the British Zone, to feed people from concentration camps and to deal with the problem of DPs (displaced persons)."

810 Military Government Bremervörde

He was governor of Zeven District, subordinate to the city of Bremervörde with Mayor Kennedy at its head. Once a week we had to report to headquarters for consultations, but fortunately we worked independently for most of the time, partly in the Zeven office, where Morrison held regular surgeries, partly travelling around, dissolving former German army camps, appointing village mayors (in some cases, such as Zeven, re-appointing old ones after denazification enquiries had been concluded), sorting out their problems, organizing ordinary food supplies or compensation claims and coping with foreign workers on farms and households. Some of these wanted to be sent home, but others did not, such as our Russian / Ukrainian families.

I do not remember all the people working at headquarters, though I knew them at the time. My impression of headquarter life was one of orgies all day and every day. Whisky galore, all free for the taking, as were cigarettes, my recently acquired addiction. It was almost impossible to tell who was drunk, doped, or naturally animated.

Mayor Kennedy was usually reclining on a couch like Goethe in Italy, with the actress Lore, his main interpreter, caressing his head and singing to him in her beautiful voice, while the woman who called herself Czech (though she was a German citizen by marriage) manicured Kennedy's toes.

21

Lore Stehn with Interpreter armband

One of the interpreters was called Anke. She had been an 'assistant' (whatever that meant) to an SS company, and I could not understand how she came to be part of the British Military Government. Instead of being grateful, she appeared to be jealous of all other interpreters and spiteful.

Three interpreters wore army uniforms: the Dutch girl Peggy, a much respected and well-liked Polish girl who was part of the Polish-British group in the army and whose name I have forgotten; and Vera, who wore the Red Army uniform, though she had long been a prisoner, working on a German farm.

Of the men I best liked Capt. Maniewski, a Polish officer who was intelligent and interesting to talk to, friendly and chivalrous in his social behaviour. Among the displaced persons he found a beautiful and charming Polish girl called Yanka. She never joined the Military Government set, but we were all delighted when they married. They rented their own flat for the duration of his work, but rarely joined the parties at headquarters. Sometimes they invited Capt. Morrison and me to their place.

Yanka and Maniewski's wedding

I also remember a good-looking Yugoslav officer, who was gallant, lively, but always a little aloof on the margin of parties, nursing a single glass of whisky all through the proceedings.

Vera and Two Captains

Capt. Laurie was a handsome young British liaison officer who lived in a house of his own in Zeven. I never quite understood his job. He travelled a great deal, and part of this was connected with Russian camps. Hence Vera often accompanied him. She spoke fluent German, and her English was no worse than mine, but, time and again, I was taken along with Vera when clear interpreting was required for Russian contacts. Vera tried to persuade the governor to let her move to Zeven, but Capt. Laurie found various arguments against such a plan.

Once Vera and I went with Captains Morrison and Laurie to the Russian camp at Seedorf, half way between Zeven and Bremervörde. Vera had been a nurse in the Soviet army when she was taken prisoner by the German troops. Theoretically

23

she was still a member of the Soviet army. They knew, and for a time approved, of her work as an interpreter, but when we went to Seedorf to solve some routine problem, Vera was called to another barrack room while we (Morrison, Laurie and I) stayed in conversation with Russian officers in the usual half-official, half-social, vodka-drinking manner. When our business was concluded, we asked for Vera and were told that she would not be coming back with us. She was going to stay with her comrades from now on. We asked to see her to discuss what to do with her personal belongings, but were told that she had already left this camp for another and would contact us later.

As we were about to get into our cars, all three of us were sure that we heard her voice calling "Captain Laurie!" from somewhere. The Russians smiled and replied that we must have a vivid imagination. We left Seedorf. After all, Vera was one of them, so we could not interfere.

But Mayor Kennedy did not agree. Those Reds could not just abduct a member of the British Military Government, he raged. He ordered three tanks to pay a visit to the camp and insist politely on hearing from Vera herself that she was going to stay there. They too were told politely that Vera was no longer at Seedorf and that the British Army should mind their own business. Then even Kennedy gave up.

A few days later – I happened to be at home with the Emdes – there came a frantic phone-call from Capt. Laurie. Vera had turned up at his house and some drunken Russian soldiers were shouting outside. Vera – we found out later – had been at Niendorf camp, where she persuaded three soldiers to come with her for a picnic and bring along some vodka. They dropped in at German inns on the way for extra drops of home-brewed liquor, and when her companions were well and truly under the influence and half asleep, Vera took over the steering wheel and drove them to Laurie's house. There they were – three rowdy soldiers outside and a female inside who was to all intents and purposes a Red Army deserter. Could I get him out of this mess? To harbour a deserter was against all diplomatic agreements. I told him that he was mad to assume that I of all people could achieve more with Vera than he, but I would contact Morrison and possibly Kennedy, even though that rash man might make the situation worse.

In the end we persuaded Vera to drive her soldiers some way back on the road they had come from; Morrison and I would pick her up at a less dangerous point. It worked, and we took Vera to my lodgings, promising that Capt. Laurie would come as soon as he had made sure there was no danger. Vera loved the drama of our whispering-hiding game, but I certainly did not enjoy my task of trying to keep her quiet in those rooms overlooking the garden. Time and again she escaped to rooms that overlooked the street, hoping to be seen, I suspected. At last Morrison arrived, without Laurie. Vera was furious, but Morrison managed to calm her. They had negotiated with Bremervörde, where Laurie was now waiting for her. She could come to him in Morrison's car, provided she crouched in the back seat and behaved well. I sat in the back with her to make sure she obeyed.

Although it was dark by then, we took a road that avoided the Seedorf camp. When we arrived at the headquarters' hotel, we found the garage doors wide open. They were closed by soldiers as soon as Morrison had driven in. We went upstairs from inside.

Kennedy received Vera like a long-lost child. He was weeping with joy and whisky. Poor kid, needing 'political' asylum in the West! She sure would get it, he, Kennedy would see to that. And Laurie was there, too, torn between feelings of responsibility and anger. We all celebrated Vera's return until it was time to depart at crack of dawn.

Capt. Laurie was taking several sacks of potatoes to friends in Belgium – he had documents entitling him to do so. Vera would be one of those sacks, in the back of his jeep, every time they had to cross a border. Morrison and I would follow as far as a place where we could overlook the bridge in Bremen where the American control post stood. Unlike the rest of North Germany, Bremen and Hamburg were part of the American Zone. Until we reached that border, Vera could travel in relative comfort in the back of Morrison's car, keeping an eye on Laurie's jeep. Before Bremen we stopped on the hard shoulder of the Autobahn and tied Vera into a sack among the other potatoes. Morrison and I watched in suspense as the American read Laurie's papers, poked a stick about in the back of the jeep and then waved them on. As the other borders were British-controlled, we sighed optimistically.

By then poor Morrison felt so exhausted, he said he would give me brief driving instructions and then let me drive him home. He slept on the passenger seat. I was glad to be of service and on this straight road without traffic it was quite easy until we approached the Sittensen exit and I did not remember – or had never been told – how to brake. I shouted for Morrison to wake up and show me. He woke and showed me how, but the car stalled. We changed seats, and I felt that I would never again learn how to drive.

Morrison was a wonderful man. He tried to keep all strenuous or depressing jobs from me. I never saw Belsen, though it was not far from us. Nor did I hear anything about concentration camps while I was with Military Government, or rather not within Military Government circles. It was the nice Zeven mayor who enlightened me, adding that Morrison did not want me to know. How crazy, when I had seen those people on the road near Danzig! It was like having an over-protective parent again, leaving me to guess at half-truths. I pleaded with Morrison to treat me like an adult. So he took me along to do the interpreting when Germans had to be forcibly evicted from a former army camp, where they had settled illegally. And all the while he kept apologizing.

So many people exploited Morrison's kindness, but he just laughed when I expressed anger. "Poor misguided souls," he said.

Sometimes I had to translate stories of suffering from persecution by the Nazis which were so obviously false they made me blush. But Morrison always showed patient understanding and seemed more sorry than angry. I was aghast when "that man", as we still called him, even though he now lived in Freyersen and we knew his name was Schulz, the one who had called me a Russian chieftain and threatened us with a gun only three months earlier, had the nerve to come to surgery with some story of his suffering under the Nazis and, worse still, with a claim for compensation. Did he not remember me? Or did he think I did not remember him when his voice and appearance were indelibly impressed on my brain? He probably did not know where I was working and kept his composure when he saw me. I owed it to Morrison to keep mine while "that man" was in the room, but as soon as he had left, I lost my temper. Morrison quietly dropped the written claim in the waste paper basket. "Forget him", he said, "an aberration like him should not soil a nice girl's memory." That was easier said than done.

Occasionally, when I was out riding, I bumped into that man and found his very appearance irritating. But he could not stop me from enjoying rides in the company of various officers from the British army.

Horses

Our horses worked for their keep on different farms, but we could still use them for riding. Word of these Trakehnen riding horses had reached the British army when they arrived in Zeven. I was glad of the company of good riders, and each was every inch a British gentleman, just as I had always imagined them and very different from Military Government personnel. One of my riding companions must have been Churchill's son-in-law Christopher Soames[3]. I cannot clearly decipher his name on a piece of paper he sent me, asking for a riding appointment, but I knew he was somehow related to Churchill, because once, when I expressed doubts about Churchill as a statesman (an opinion recently acquired in political discussions on those rare occasions when Military Government officers were sober), my riding companion firmly told me that I was wrong and that he knew better as a close relative of the great man. I accepted his judgement with an embarrassed blush. Maybe Churchill was greater than we thought and not simply a good orator and rabble-rouser as Hitler had been?

I gave this man permission to ride our horses when I was away. Morrison had been transferred to Oldenburg and Aurich in Friesland and I had agreed to go with him if Edith Massmann could also have a job there. Edith was exceedingly pleased to leave her all too lively and artistic mother and stepfather and her little step-brother in Beuel, near Bad Godesberg. Her parents were divorced, and her father was a very sober GP practising in Mühlhausen in the Ruhrgebiet. Some years later he came to visit me in London and took me on a trail in Edgar Wallace's footsteps, culminating in my being thrown out of the Old Bailey, where I had interpreted the proceedings for him. During our walk around town Dr Massmann also invited me for tea at the Ritz, but he found the service impossibly arrogant and we moved on to the Waldorf Astoria instead. But at the time when Edith came to Friesland, I had not yet met her father.

Before travelling to Friesland, I spent a week with Mutti. Somehow one of my soldier admirers from Summer 1944, Karl-Heinz Caspari, had found our address and, after his safe return from the war, came to visit us. He seemed to blame my reluctance to be nice, let alone loving, on a certain hangover after a traumatic year, and so he kept in touch despite my rebuffs. I knew that he had found some job in a much-acclaimed theatre in Bonn; but it was not until I visited Edith that I

---

[3] Actually, this must have been Peregrine Worsthorne, who later became editor of the Sunday Telegraph. Churchill's wife, Clementine Hozier, was the aunt of Worsthorne's wife, Lucinda Hozier.

understood that Caspari had become a household name to German theatre-lovers. He directed, acted and wrote his own plays, which reminded me a bit of the poems he had once written for me.

Note from Peregrine Worsthorne

My journey to Bad Godesberg was every bit as difficult as that journey from Ebersbach to Mikalbude had been in December 1944: hanging on to a hand rail on the footstep of a train, hitch-hiking in British lorries. There followed a life of luxury at Edith's mother's home, reminiscing and planning for the future.

Just before we were due to travel to Oldenburg, Vera turned up. She had discovered that those Belgian friends of Capt. Laurie's to whose care he had entrusted this 'political refugee from Russia' were in fact the family of Laurie's fiancée. Vera was not having any of that. It was HER Capt. Laurie! Alas, he was no longer in Zeven. Morrison was inclined to let Vera fend for herself, but Kennedy was scared of a political scandal which might highlight his own part in sheltering a Red Army deserter; or indeed Vera might even have claimed that we had abducted her. So Morrison was given the task of keeping her in hiding "until we can contact Capt. Laurie", she was told.

She received a German identity card with the name of Frieda somebody-or-other. The adventure appealed to her. But the sheltered home of Dr Ahnert, the mother of Hedy, a former roommate of Edith's in a Prague students' hostel, did not please Vera / Frieda at all, although it was a comfortable, friendly household in Oldenburg.

27

When we took Vera out to parties, she was certainly Frieda. Her German was free of any accent.

During the day, when Hedy's mother was busy with her surgery and we went to the office, Vera walked around shops, or in the park, chatting to people. One day we all visited the highly eccentric home of an old friend of Hedy's mother, whose name was Steiner. She was some relation of Rudolf Steiner (for a time I thought she was his widow, but if so, she must have been at least twenty years younger than he had been.) Vera found her place very exciting with all those wall hangings, curtains coming from the ceiling in unexpected places, Buddha statues, Picasso paintings and the owner walking around in long gowns, offering us tea.

But most days were dull for Vera, particularly after Edith and I took a room in Aurich, where we worked in the office all day and played poker with Morrison every evening. I too could have died of boredom.

Whenever we visited Oldenburg, Dr Ahnert expressed concern about Vera going out with American soldiers, joking about her name "Frieda", sometimes returning home late and drunk, shouting across the street "Try and guess my real name. Guess my nationality." We talked to her and she promised to be good and patient until Laurie came. But one day she had bolted with all her luggage and more. Several months later somebody told us that Vera was seen with a Russian boyfriend at a barn dance in one of the little villages, smothered in make-up and apparently happy.

Morrison too enjoyed barn dances in Freyersen and relaxation from his mostly strenuous, sometimes quite absurd work. He had to deal with complaints about theft and denunciations of black-marketeers. "Those poor people", he called them; "like hell", I thought. Some, wanting a special favour from Morrison, tried to bribe me with items like eggs for my family. Others said "As a German, you must want to help me"… to get this or that privilege. I remember a German girl appearing with a French prisoner-of-war. "We would like to get married, *Herr Gouverneur*," she said in German. The man asked if we understood French and then explained that he merely wished to be repatriated, not to be married. Could we explain that to his girlfriend?

I also remember the nice mayor of Zeven jumping to his feet when Morrison entered, automatically raising his arm and calling *"Heil Hitler!"* Then he stammered in embarrassment.

A familiar story, told to us again and again, was that of denouncing house owners as ex-Nazis whose property should be requisitioned and given to refugees "who never had anything to do with the Nazis". And who could prove if they had or had not? There were no documents left from those far-away places from which we came.

Und so finden wir uns wieder in dem heitern bunten Reihn,
Und es soll der Kranz der Lieder frisch und grün geflochtne sein.

Aber wem der Götter bringen wir des Liedes ersten Zoll?
Ihm vor allen lasst uns singen, der die Freude schaffen soll.

Denn was frommt es, dass mit Leben Ceres den Altar geschmückt?
Dass den Purpursaft der Reben Bacchus in die Schale drückt?

Zuckt vom Himmel nicht der Funken, der den Herd in Flammen setzt:
Ist der Geist nicht freudetrunken, und das Herz bleibt umergötzt.

Aus den Wolken muss es fallen, aus der Götter Schoß das Glück,
Und der mächtigste von allen Herrschern ist der Augenblick.

Von dem allerersten Werden der unendlichen Natur,
Alles Göttliche auf Erden ist ein Lichtgedanke nur.

Langsam in dem Lauf der Horen fuget sich der Stein zum Stein:
Schnell, wie es der Geist geboren, will das Werk empfunden sein.

Wie im hellen Sonnenblicke sich ein Farbenteppich webt,
Wie auf ihrer bunten Brücke Iris durch den Himmel schwebt,

So ist jede schöne Gabe flüchtig wie des Blitzes Schein;
Schnell in ihrem düstern Grabe schließt die Nacht sie wieder ein.

We find ourselves again 'midst colours bright and gay,
With songs that weave a wreath, a fresh and green array.

But to which of all the gods shall we offer the first tune?
Let's sing at first to him who'll bring pleasure to us soon.

For what's the use of Ceres showing life upon the shrine?
Or Bacchus filling bowls with juice of the purple vine?

Does not the spark that lights the hearth come down from heaven's height?
Do not our hearts exult in joy, our spirits then take flight?

From clouds above descends this joy, a true divine bestowment,
For the mightiest ruler of them all is this: each unique moment.

From the very earliest inklings of unending nature's birth,
All that's godly is no more than a flash upon our earth.

The Moirai weave their web, slowly stones fuse into one,
Yet art seeks release from the heart as soon as it's begun

As a coloured carpet's born from dazzling Apollo's gleam,
Or Iris floats twixt earth and heav'n on her radiant sunbeam

And each gift flees as quickly as Jove's angry flash of light
Until engulfed again, so soon, by deadly shades of night

(Schiller, Die Gunst des Augenblicks)

Tristan

By the time Morrison was demobbed and the Oldenburg-Aurich offices closed we had still not heard from Tristan Jones. So Edith and I hitch-hiked from Aurich to Zeven. For some stupid reason we had not taken our after-curfew passes, and as it grew dark, there seemed to be a number of Military Police on the roads. We managed to dodge them, but when we eventually reached Zeven at 3 a.m. we felt exhausted. We could not face the road to Freyersen, and I could only think of one family who were still likely to be awake – a mother with two grown-up daughters who lived almost opposite the Dr Schaper house that had once been requisitioned for Morrison. The women were reputed to be running their own 3-woman brothel, but I did not really know what a brothel was and had always found these women kind and friendly. So we knocked at their door and were welcomed. It was quite an experience to spend a night in a brothel, though we were generously given space on the fringe of the goings-on, in a far corner of their one and only bedroom. There was a big breakfast party in the late morning, big in terms of numbers of people and lavish food. They were too kind and generous to accept money from us. Not that German money was worth anything, anyhow. We, equally generously, received and reciprocated farewell hugs and kisses.

The other memorable event of that day was that, after the long walk to Freyersen, Edith and I managed to eat an entire big basket full of mushrooms which Mutti had just picked in fields and forest. She kept preparing one large frying pan full after another, expecting us to be sick any time; she simply could not refuse our pleas for more.

While still secretly hoping to hear about a newspaper job I applied for one as an interpreter-secretary at the garrison engineer's office in Zeven. It was interesting, to the extent that it was an opportunity to discover how much boredom one could survive. Then Tristan Jones wrote to say he would collect Edith and subsequently me on his way to their new offices in Lübeck. The garrison engineer asked me to look for a replacement before I left. That was easy. Our former East Prussian neighbour Anneliese Bagdahn was thrilled at the prospect of such a 'chic' job. She had just married by correspondence her fiancé from the time when she studied English and Spanish in Hamburg. He was an officer in the German merchant navy and had landed in Brazil. I wondered why he could not come back to Germany. He never saw his mother again, yet marriage by proxy suited him. I thought it was a big gamble to marry a man whom she had only known for one year, several years ago; but Anneliese thought it wonderful that this naval officer – like most officers – had remained faithful. She was looking forward to a good life in South America, but meanwhile she was hoping for a bit of fun with the Brits.

Edith arrived from Godesberg in an armed car together with Tristan Jones and Del ('Jim') Flatley, the *News Guardian* crime reporter who had secured their greatest scoop in October 1945 by interviewing a source close to Eva Braun, and obtaining an exclusive picture of her. Another armoured car came along and together – Edith and I hiding at the bottom of the vehicle – we crossed the tricky bridge in Hamburg where controls were supposed to be very strict. It was almost as exciting as Vera's Bremen crossing in the potato sack.

News Guardian scoop on Eva Braun

The News Guardian clippings show:

The **News Guardian**

Eva Braun—Hitler's Mistress For 19 Years

Godesberg Confidante Arrested

"LIBERAL" JAP CABINET PLEDGED

The **News Guardian** ★ PICTURE ★ SUPPLEMENT

I'm no Angel! *Eva Braun*

Lübeck – the News Guardian

In Lübeck Tristan had managed to rent a large, sunny room for us at the house of a well-off dairy owner called Dreger. The house was on a small rising on the outskirts of the town, in Overbek Strasse. In this small Hanseatic town even the longest distances were short. We loved our room and the kind owners who in turn loved us for saving them from the fate of having rooms requisitioned for "dirty refugees". The expression made me wince. It was sad that everybody loathed the refugee peril.

Tristan was taken aback when he discovered that Mrs and Miss Dreger's favourite writer was Galsworthy. He had previously told us that they were very educated people. He spent hours talking with them about literature, tactfully, patiently, and very pedantically extolling the merits of other writers without much success.

Tristan was undoubtedly the best educated member of the paper's staff. People kept telling Edith and me that they had seen the letters MA behind his name on job application forms. In reality Tristan had never been awarded his MA at Oxford, though in theory every Oxford BA acquires an MA if he pays a sum of money. Tristan would not do that; but since he deserved the MA, he used the letters occasionally. We learnt all that later. For the time being such things meant nothing to us, but we realized that Tristan was somehow important. He certainly was the de facto editor, while the nominal editor, Capt. Maxwell Scott[4], was an enthusiastic journalist figurehead, wanting to learn from his assistant, Corporal Jones. To me it seemed strange how Tristan, so very imaginative himself, would not leave anything to the imagination of readers, but insisted on spelling things out, A, B, C fashion, as if addressing children. I found it irritating when he added pedantic explanations to any feature I wrote. I learnt a great deal of correct English from the way he re-wrote my articles, but nothing sounded in the least like the ideas I had in mind when I started to write. At least I was generally credited (as AW), although it was not until 1949 that I got my first byline. Tristan's own articles were generally anonymous; sometimes we just used 'special reporter'.

Working through the night on the rotary press

---

[4] Later Sir Michael Fergus Maxwell Scott, 13th Baronet; he died in 1989.

News Guardian office and editorial desk

It did not matter much, as I was rarely asked to write features. Most of my writing was as a film critic, summarizing the plots of films available for the entertainment of the British Army of the Rhine and such lucky Germans as had a British press pass. I often thought of Gisela and how she would have enjoyed my job. But Gisela was dead. Armand Claussin had written about her, avoiding details. They, the Belgian ex-prisoners had been repatriated from East Prussia, not by the shortest route across Germany, but all the way via the Black Sea. It had been a long and hard journey which seemed to confirm all their anti-Russian, or rather anti-Slav, prejudices. And there, somewhere in the middle of European Russia, Gisela and her mother had also been together with many other German women. "The thought of you, too, being treated like that, constantly weighed on our minds and frightened us," Claussin wrote. Then he added that Gisela's mother managed to commit suicide after she had witnessed her daughter's horrible death. "The sins of our fathers…", I thought. It was not fair that I was not made to pay in any way. Why was I so lucky? Tristan, of course, said that the Belgians were taken to the Black Sea in order to show them the lovely country… and that the report of Gisela's death was probably largely exaggerated. Lord forgive the bias of a communist, I thought.

The News Guardian

Demob Edition, 29 May 1946, p. 2

* Vitya *
A child of the war

Veteran members of 32 Guards Brigade HQ, and particularly members of the mixed independent recce group known as "Ward Force," may remember this little Russian boy whom they met in the village of Freyersen, near Zeven, which they entered on 19 April 1945. This is his story, the story of Vitya Vladimirovitch Mosin, a child of the war.

The Stalingrad disaster was over. Step by step, the German troops retreated towards their own frontiers, abandoning the vast Russian countryside and leaving behind them a fiery trail of blazing villages and homesteads.

Everything that might be of use to the pursuing Red Army must be destroyed.

Manpower, too, must be removed. Vast congregations of peasants and townspeople were driven before them.

Among them Vladimir Markovitch Mosin, headmaster of a high school near Moscow.

Vladimir Markovitch and his father, Mark Petrovitch and his little boy, Viktor – "Vitya".

The slave workers reached Mickelau, an estate in East Prussia which the Soviet Union was later to take within its own borders.

It was late evening. Wrapped in tattered clothes which once he had been proud to wear, Vitya, three years old, sat on the edge of a farm cart. The war had been his life. He was destined to know little of peace.

"What a comic little brat. Look how his belly is swollen – and how thin his arms and legs are. That's not a healthy child!"

Contemptuously the Germans compared him with their own children.

"It just shows – the Russians don't even know how to feed their own kids."

Vladimir Markovitch listened in amazement. He knew enough German to grasp the meaning of their remarks.

"Don't know how to feed their children?"

***

The past, which now seemed so far away, leapt back at him. He saw himself, headmaster of his school, coming home after the day's work was done.

His five children were playing ball, the older ones laughing at Vitya, who was so annoyed at his inability to throw the ball like the rest of them.

The child had run towards him as fast as his chubby little legs would carry him.

"Oh, Daddy, they're laughing at me. But I'll soon be as big as they are, won't I?"

"Sure you will, if you always eat carrots and do what mother says. Come on, children, I think dinner must be ready."

And five healthy children, with giant appetites, sat down at the table.

The dream gave way to another picture, a picture from the far more recent past.

Vitya was sitting on the same farm-cart as now, impatiently asking:

"Why don't we go home? I'm so hungry and Mama will be waiting for us."

But his father could not speak. How could he tell his son:

"We are home, Vitya; at least, this was our home two days ago. And Mama is not waiting for us. She – and Grandmama and your brothers and sisters are dead – burnt to death."

Utterly dazed, they had obeyed the orders of the invader. A journey which was to last eight months began.

They were completely exhausted. Bomb from the Luftwaffe, the daily sight of their countrymen dying, dead Germans, curses and shouts – what did it all matter?

Nothing mattered – nothing except potatoes and milk, milk and potatoes, occasionally a bowl of soup or a crust of bread.

Life was over, but the stomach would not die.

"They don't even know how to feed their children."

***

Vladimir Markovitch smiled bitterly. So here they were – his family; his old father and that little bundle of humanity with the swollen belly, the dangling legs and the dark, glazed eyes that recalled the eyes of dying men.

A woman brought the child a piece of cake and a cup of milk. But he had learned to trust no-one. He pushed the cake away, spat in the milk and clung, howling, to his father, burying his head in his coat.

"What a spoilt child! In Germany we bring children up better than that."

Only the landowner's little dachshund failed to see at once that Vitya Vladimirovitch was a hopelessly ill-bred child. The dog jumped into the cart and started licking his little hands. Vitya appreciated this gesture of friendship and shouted for joy:

"Daddy, look! He's tickling me – but it's a nice dog, isn't it, Daddy?"

But no sooner had pleasure shown itself on his face than it vanished again, as if he realized that this world was no place for laughter.

One person only in that crowd of foreigners was moved to pity. Tears came to the eyes of a young girl, daughter of the landowner, for she wanted so much to help, but had little idea of how to do it.

Very quietly, in the few words of Russian that she knew, she spoke to him:

"That's your dog, Vitya. Do you like it very much?"

And the boy replied:

"Yes, I do, Mama, but…"

He stopped, shocked at the word he had used and gazed helplessly at the girl he had called "Mama".

She came closer. Suddenly he flung his arms round her neck and asked:

"Do you like me?"

***

The months which followed brought him some happiness. The gardens, the fields and the farmhouse were his playground; his little dog was his companion. Slowly the horrors of war began to fade in his memory.

The child was extremely intelligent and, as his health returned, good-looking.

Vladimir Markovitch dare to hope again.

"When the war is over, if Vitya is still alive and healthy – then at least there's some future for us."

Yet he remained suspicious and afraid. Here was he, a slave in a foreign land, unable to control his own or his son's life. What if the German girl were to say one day:

"I'm tired of looking after the boy. Take him to work with you and look after him yourself?"

And if Vitya's 'Mama' abandoned him, would it not in one blow destroy that confidence in people which had so painfully been restored in him?

His suspicions were increased when he noticed that, with obvious haste, the girl was making all kinds of clothes for the child – enough to last him a year at least.

***

"Poor Vitya," he thought. "Little do you realize that your 'Mama' has lost her first enthusiasm, has forgotten the pity she once felt for you. You are fond of her, even when, for reasons she will never tell you, she forbids you to play with the German children. But the time is coming when she will hand me the clothes and say: 'I've done what I could. Now you must look after him'."

The truth was otherwise and only three people knew it – the girl, her father and the District Leader of the Nazi Party.

The latter had, in fact, already written to Koch, Gauleiter of East Prussia and exploiter-in-chief of the Ukraine, denouncing this girl who adopted a Russian child and who had frequently been observed discussing private affairs with a Russian slave-worker.

Only these three, two of them fearing, one of them hoping for the arrival of the Gestapo's car to remove 'Mama' to a place where she could concentrate her thoughts on her lack of patriotism, realized why she had knitted and sewed with such feverish haste, why she tried to avoid trouble for the German children by forbidding Vitya to play with them.

But instead of the expected order from the Gestapo, a very different order came to Mickelau:

"The Bolshevist Hordes are approaching. The civilian population must evacuate the district. Those who refuse to leave will be considered friends of the enemy and will be shot as such by the Volkssturm. Foreign workers are also to be evacuated."

Again a journey – three months this time – and again the farm-cart. Food was as scarce as before. Chaos reigned on the roads of a Germany going down to defeat. But this time there was no apathy, no resignation to fate, in the little family.

Instead, Grandfather Mark Petrovitch asserted:

"God has saved this little boy through all this trouble, when so many others have been killed. God has saved our Vitya. Surely a better future awaits us? We must be patient – that's all."

***

In a little village near Zeven, a village which was the Headquarters for a few days of 32nd Guards Brigade, the family of Vladimir Markovitch heard the news that the war was over.

They had reached the end of their journey a bare six weeks before the Guards Division entered the village on April 19. The little Russian quickly found friends amongst the British soldiers. They gave him sweets and chocolate and, at least, he could play with the other children.

"God has preserved our Vitya for a better future," Grandpa said again.

Five months later Vitya was removed from a camp for Displaced Persons to a DP Ward in a German hospital. He had contracted scarlet fever. His heart, strained with the sufferings of four years of war, was too weak to repel the attack. On 3 September he was dead.

The German hospital authorities told his father and his 'Mama' two days later. They had brought clean clothes and fresh fruit "for some Russian kid in the DP Ward."

A.W.

In most respects life at the paper was fun, companionship better than any I had experienced. Drinking was a very minor social aspect, just the odd beer. Never before had I come across such dry, straight-faced humour, the way these soldiers dropped the punch-line of a joke quite casually while they went on telling the story that had already finished. All this was so fast, that by the time I could laugh the delayed reaction became a joke in itself. Yet the soldiers thought that Edith and I were the ones to talk so fast in German that we could not have time to breathe.

Lübeck Legends: an article by 'A.W.' in the News Guardian
'"Gustav", she said to him one day' was 'improved' by Tristan

When Norman was chosen to go to Berlin, I joined him in Russian lessons in the hope that learning to read might help me to retain what I had learnt orally from Vitya and the other Russians on our farm. Norman and I spent pleasant long evenings swotting over those difficult letters and discussing our ideas of the Soviet Union. Later he sent me a letter from Berlin which included a photo of himself with two Russian soldier friends. He was determined to persevere with the language, but I gave up.

Norman continuing his Russian studies

Tristan and one of the printing workers by the name of David McKenzie were among the first to be demobbed. David came from Arbroath, which was not far from Friockheim, where we knew Claus to be a prisoner-of-war. He was going to invite him to his home. Tristan also wanted to visit Claus and to take him presents. Claus specially wanted logarithm tables.

Soon after Tristan left, the paper disbanded, but the remaining staff did not. We ate big breakfasts in the canteen, then played Bridge for an hour or so. Then we went ice skating, which was hilarious, as none of the British soldiers had ever done it before. Back to the canteen for what Tristan used to call lunch and the others called dinner. Back to the ice rink, with music in the afternoon. Later in the evening we returned to the canteen for tea and more Bridge. When Rita came to visit us from Hamburg, Bridge playing was replaced by listening to Boogie-Woogie, Tiger Rag, Bach, Beethoven, sometimes Chopin. Then Bridge again until sometime after midnight, when the sergeant had gone to bed and we raided the pantry for tins of peaches for a midnight feast. All this, and chain smoking, we kept up for more than a month without being really bored. We were always escorted home in the early hours. Only once did I interrupt the routine, when Karl-Heinz Caspari came to visit me for a day. He tried to make love to me in my Dreger room, but though I felt very sorry for him, I just could not oblige.

My best companions were Cliff (Arthur Clifford) and Bill. Cliff had been the paper's news editor, and as he always had the radio roaring at full volume while he was doing his typing, I once took him to a German doctor who specialized in ear disorders. He decided that Cliff's ears needed syringing, and after that the office radio in the news editor's room became very quiet. Cliff also had a marvellous sense of humour and I liked him very much. He had a beautiful girlfriend at home with whom he was constantly at war, but I was sure that he loved her.

Bill had no other attachments. Tristan had always said that he himself dearly loved his wife Mary, who had a wartime job at the Craven A factory and kept sending him large parcels of those cigarettes. Her picture constantly adorned one of Tristan's shelves, just as, or even more constantly than, Beryl adorned Cliff's room. But after he was demobbed Tristan kept sending me regular long letters which frightened me. I decided that the best way to put a stop to this was to become officially engaged to Bill. He was such a pleasant man, a designer by profession, and Mutti, Omi and Marlene liked him nearly as much as they liked Tristan. I still cannot understand why this engagement did not work out.

By spring all the former News Guardian staff had left and the print works had been handed back to the German owners.

Edith and I found a new job at the Transit Hotel. This job was moderately challenging, as we were expected to look cheerful after a 12-hour working day, supposedly simply sitting behind the desk in the entrance hall, but more often climbing up and down high flights of stairs, showing visitors their rooms. These visitors were quite interesting people, writers, artists, business men. One of our jobs was to keep the reception area tidy, for instance to sort out golf clubs that had been dumped and fallen out of their bags. I had never before seen a golf club, but here everyone, including the female guests, seemed to own a set.

To the extent of becoming familiar with supposedly famous names and faces our job was quite interesting. We knew the tastes in wine and food of the more regular visitors, and the mess they did or did not make of their bedrooms. We judged their personalities according to the tips they gave to chambermaids and waiters. We at reception were treated as ladies and not given tips, worse luck. We worked a flexible 6-day week and on our days off we went out with whichever waiter happened to be free. The head waiter was a Berliner who step-danced to the dining room singing a pop-song, but became totally dignified and sedate when he approached a guest's table. He painted the world in blacker than black colours and bounced back on this black wall with great energy and laughter. That particular Berlin brand of humour was indeed a recipe for Berlin's post-war survival. I was soon to experience Berlin first-hand.

To Berlin with the Stephens family

It must have been Tristan who gave Mr Stephens my address, because I heard that Tristan was now working at The Observer and the Jones family were close friends of David Astor, now editor. David's name had cropped up once before, on a heady night in Hamburg when Tristan and I had met Marion Gräfin Dönhoff to hand over some money raised for the widows and orphans of the Adam von Trott assassination attempt on Hitler. Christabel Bielenberg had created a 20th July Memorial Fund, money had poured in following two advertisements in The Observer and The Times, and David had entrusted Tristan with passing it to the countess, to hand to the families concerned. I recall her driving us back to Weertzen in her open-top Porsche, talking all the time about her firm belief that we'd all be returning to East Prussia eventually. Omi was always saying similar things – her confidence had been part of the reason she had agreed to leave our horses with various farmers on the trek west, assuming we could pick them up again on the return journey – so this was music to her ears. But I had my doubts, and Mutti too.

Mr Stephens often had to visit the press headquarters in Frankfurt, though mainly working in Berlin as the foreign correspondent for The Observer. Chris Bielenberg also worked as his assistant. He said he would like to interview me with regard to a job as secretary / translator / reporter on German affairs. I thought that was a joke, as I could neither type, nor speak good English and my reporting experience consisted of 'what's on at the local flicks'. But Mr Stephens accepted me, probably thinking it wise to have an inoffensive person like me. And so began the best time of my post-war life.

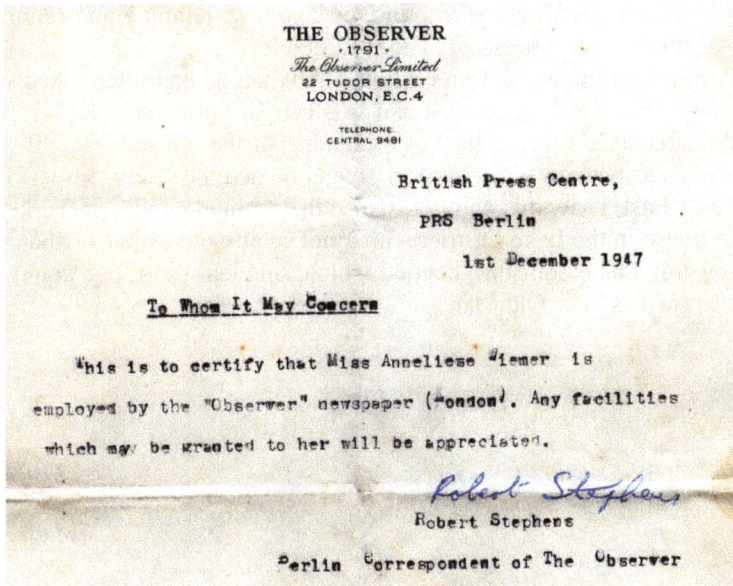

THE OBSERVER
· 1791 ·
The Observer Limited
22 TUDOR STREET
LONDON, E.C.4

TELEPHONE
CENTRAL 9481

British Press Centre,

PRS Berlin

1st December 1947

To Whom It May Concern

This is to certify that Miss Anneliese Siemer is employed by the "Observer" newspaper (London). Any facilities which may be granted to her will be appreciated.

Robert Stephens

Robert Stephens

Berlin Correspondent of The Observer

A press pass, of sorts

The Berlin experience was threefold. First, there were the Berliners, a complete contrast to the ever-moaning, lethargic West Germans. They were rebuilding their lives with individual initiatives before there was any official guidance, extracting from the rubble of former houses anything that could be put to good use. Black markets thrived quite openly.

Secondly there were the four occupation powers competing with the latest their countries could show in terms of culture. My press pass opened doors to Russian operas and ballets, allowing me to sit in VIP boxes with communist leaders such as Piek and Grotewohl and sometimes the Russian commander Sokolovsky. Doors opened to the American show piece, Thornton Wilder's 'Our Town'; Yehudi Menuhin performing for the British and Britten's 'Peter Grimes' having its premiere in Berlin; and best of all, the première of 'Les Mouches'. On the German side Brecht was starting at the Schiffbauerdamm theatre.

41

But more important than any of those experiences was that of working for the Stephenses. I had never known people who argued passionately their views on art, politics, poetry economics, music, without ever appearing to wish to convert others, indeed never opposing the opposite. The large circle of their friends reflected their own tolerance: Palestinian refugees like the Bushnaks, Israelis like Lotte Geiger or even ardent Zionists, for instance. I heard of and later met in person Mr Stephens' wonderful widowed mother, who had worked in a factory to give her son an education and who lived in a basement flat in Camden Town where the smell of fried bacon lingered all day and a huge kettle was kept on the boil over an open cooking range in preparation for possible callers. Mr Stephens' sisters lived there, drying their hair in curlers, or manicuring their hands while a happy crowd of ever so many young children were screaming, or laughing, jumping and running; and where everything was spotless, tidy and respectable.

Bob Stephens had married Taqui Altounyan when he had hitch-hiked with his previous fiancée to the Middle East and was caught up in Jerusalem in the war, writing first freelance reports, then as a member of the 'Observer' staff. Taqui's family lived in a spacious house in Aleppo and owned the second largest hospital in the Middle East. I saw this on photos, also their mountain villa in Turkey and a very large house in the Lake District with a not so attractive annexe and a garden sloping towards Lake Coniston, beyond which, on clear days, one could see the mountain known as 'The Old Man'.

Nicky, Taqui and Chimpy in Berlin

Taqui was one quarter-Armenian, unconventional upper class, artistic and intellectual, untidy to the extreme, at the same time extremely concerned with hygiene and fresh air. The latter concern made me shiver in their flat, where windows were always open at opposite sides 'for a healthy through-draught'. Two-and-a-half-year-old Roger, whom we called Chimpy, was well educated in questions of draughts, and called cheerfully "Chimpy makes healthy draught" when he had farted. I thought all this was a little extreme, but was rapidly learning to appreciate the Stephenses' tolerance.

Denn schnell und spurlos geht des Mimen Kunst,
Die wunderbare, an dem Sinn vorüber,
Wenn das Gebild des Meißels, der Gesang
Des Dichters nach Jahrtausenden noch leben.
Hier stirbt der Zauber mit dem Künstler ab,
Und wie der Klang verhallet in dem Ohr,
Verrauscht des Augenblicks geschwinde Schöpfung,
Und ihren Ruhm bewahrt kein dauernd Werk.
Schwer ist die Kunst, vergänglich ist ihr Preis,
Dem Mimen flicht die Nachwelt keine Kränze;
Drum muß er geizen mit der Gegenwart,
Den Augenblick, der sein ist, ganz erfüllen,
Muß seiner Mitwelt mächtig sich versichern
Und im Gefühl der Würdigsten und Besten
Ein lebend Denkmal sich erbaun – So nimmt er
Sich seines Namens Ewigkeit voraus,
Denn wer den Besten seiner Zeit genug
Gethan, der hat gelebt für alle Zeiten.

For the wonders of the mime's art quickly, without trace, pass our senses by,
Whereas chiselled images and the songs of poets still live after millennia.
Here, magic dies with the artist, and as sounds fade from the ear,
Swift creations of the moment too wither, no lasting works preserve their fame.
Art is burdensome, its prize but fleeting; posterity weaves the mime no wreaths.
Thus she must be miserly with the moment, fill each minute that is hers,
Ensure her standing with those around, and build herself a living monument
From the feelings of the finest and most worthy amongst them.
By this means only she earns eternity for her name,
For those who do enough for the best of their own time
Will live on through perpetuity.

Schiller (Wallenstein)

My letters, October – November 1947

From the day I started my Observer job, I wrote enthusiastic letters to my mother. They read like a diary, combining cryptic notes and long descriptions.

Essen, Friday 9.15 a.m.

Dear Mamushka,

I just woke up and looked out of my large window: wonderful red maple for as far as I can see! I am thinking of yesterday and of expectations for today and must write before I boil over and die of pleasure. You must have signs of life from me, now that I have entered paradise.

On Wednesday Mr Stephens came to Lübeck and took me to Hamburg straight away. I spent the night at the Eggers. Rita had gone to Blankenese with little Christian, so I did not see them, but Mr Eggers looked after me and showed me his recent photos.

I had arranged to meet Mr Stephens at the Hauptbahnhof at 9 a.m. and hoped to see you there before. But though I waited from 8.30, there was no sign of you. Where were you? I did not have time to search Altstädterstrasse.

Then we were off in the direction of the Ruhr area.

Mr Stephens first offered me sandwiches, as he did not know I had breakfasted at the Eggers. Then he offered a cigarette. He always does that when he is smoking, even when he comes out from somewhere with a half-finished cigarette in his mouth, but I do not always accept, because I am afraid he might sack me when I become too expensive. Anyhow, the kind of conversations this man has with me, or with others, while I am listening, are too exciting to think of smoking.

I hope to God that I can somehow avoid Charles and John contacting me in Berlin. I would die of shame for being acquainted with such vulgar businessmen, if Mr Stephens were to meet them.

Mr Stephens must have masses of books, novels too, in English or French and he said that I would be allowed to read them all. He said he will read a French one (Proust) together with me. "I don't mean that you could not read it by yourself, but I thought it may be a little easier for both of us, if we did it together," he suggested. Isn't that absolutely heavenly?

We also discussed the article he wrote last night about the CCG[5]. I am no longer the least bit scared of him and do not hesitate to ask when I don't understand something.

By the way, he once called me 'Anneli' instead of 'Miss Wiemer', so I think we are becoming friends, unless to him it is a way of addressing an inferior employee.

During our journey we stopped several times at the most beautiful places to have sandwiches and admire the countryside. At such stops Mr Stephens is particularly nice, also to Pohlman, our chauffeur.

---

[5] Control Commission for Germany: the British apparatus for administering its own zone.

Mr Stephens is an extraordinary man indeed, even his lavatory habits amaze me. Unlike most men I have known, who had to run to the toilet every hour or so, hr did not go all day, even when we stopped at some sort of canteen near the motorway.

And Westphalia is a surprisingly beautiful area!

Now comes the climax: I was taken to stay with the family of the editor of 'Die Welt' who at the moment is British. I was given a beautiful bedroom of my own, with a good bed, central heating and – wonder of wonders – hot water in the taps! So I had a really good wash and change of clothes, then a short chat with Mrs Barnetson. Mr Stephens had already left.

For dinner we had soup, fish, carrots… and a dessert! Then tea and cigarettes in another room where another 'Welt' journalist joined us. Soft background radio music was supposed to enhance the interesting conversation.

Mrs Barnetson comes from Edinburgh and is the first really pretty British woman I have seen. She is also a charming hostess, as in 'good' German houses, and she has even studied at a university. Can you imagine how wonderful it all was? After the others had left, Mrs B. and I had a cup of cocoa. Then I enjoyed a proper, hot, big bath and bed. What a luxurious existence!

Now I must hurry for breakfast before going with Mr Stephens to attend a secret session of the Landtag, something like a state parliament, certainly not the federal parliament. The meeting was scheduled for Düsseldorf in preparation for tomorrow's [Lord] Packenham visit, concerning lists for dismantling industries. On Sunday night I shall be on my way to Berlin.

Bubbling over with excitement and a thousand greetings from the luckiest of all people, your Anneli

P.S. Please show this letter to Edith for her information in case she comes to Berlin with Charles and John on Thursday. Enjoy your trip with them, Mamushka.

P.P.S., later in the evening: We have come back from Düsseldorf & Solingen / Ohligs. Had tea here. Mrs Barnetson has gone away, so I will read until she returns and we can have our usual evening chat.

Mr Stephens is much more like an author and poet than a journalist. He cannot stand the sloppy way in which journalists improvise, he is very concerned with clarity and facts. How lucky I am to work with such a man! I think I will go crazy with joy. I shall learn real wisdom if this goes on and might even become an educated person after a time of working with Mr Stephens. – As he does not like hot lunches, we went to a Düsseldorf park with sandwiches, enjoyed the beauty of trees and talked poetry, philosophy and journalism.

I can't send you this letter until Mr Stephens can get an envelope, so I might write a little more before going to Berlin.

Ohligs Press Club, Saturday lunchtime. Now I have an envelope, so here just quickly are some bits of news:

Last evening I read a book about British social history. Don't worry, it's not socialist, but social. The Barnetsons are very conservative, actually capitalists in a way, though neither by birth, nor of the nouveau-rich type. We were visited by Mr Haines to discuss printing-and distribution problems of 'Die Welt'. We had supper with him before the Barnetsons came back, then tea and conversation in the drawing room. We heard beautiful waltzes on the radio; I told them how much I loved dancing, so we danced. At 8.30 p.m. Mrs Barnetson came back and Haines had to go back to the office. Mrs B. and I first had another pot of tea, then cocoa again and talked till midnight. Once again I indulged in a deep hot bath.

Mr Stephens arrived when I was still having breakfast. We went for a talk with a German economics expert about the demolition problems. He represented the 'Ministerpräsident' and spoke fluent English. So there was not much work for me. I am just receiving presents, mainly the chance to learn.

Mr Stephens treated me ever so politely. He always opened car doors for me to get in or out of the car.

Later that afternoon, back in Ohligs

I must find time to tell you more about Lord Packenham. He seemed ever such a nice, genuine person and so idealistic, that I felt he was in the wrong job as a politician. Mr Stephens could probably do a better job, but it was interesting to watch the audience's reaction to Packenham. Comments by the Minister for Economic Affairs of Nordrhein-Westfalen more or less summarized the general consensus on Packenham, that he would make a better priest than a politician. A Swiss journalist stated that only a strong personality like Churchill could manage these complicated German problems and still retain respect, even affection from German people. He may be, repeat 'may be', right. I can hardly wait to read the treatment of his speech in Monday's press.

Mr Barnetson had gone to Scotland, where his father had died. Mr Stephens stayed for coffee and cake and later, Mrs Barnetson and I had our usual midnight session.

Berlin, Sunday night

We had a marvellous journey, taking only seven hours from Essen to here. Russians at the border were very funny: I had to go inside with my passport and visa. One of the Russians said that I should send those English packing and stay with them, krisziva, he addressed me. The other man was annoyed. "That one krisziva?", he said "Niet, niet, not beautiful at all. She'd better be off with the English."

At the Helmstedt canteen we took food and a little lap-table for the car. And then we played – don't laugh, Mamushka – chess; yes, me playing chess! I did not actually show that kind of patient tolerance that the game required, but Mr Stephens made up for my failings. I would have liked to be better in order to give Mr Stephens a more interesting game, but maybe he did find it challenging to anticipate my unpredictable moves, and once I even won a game by mistake.

I had never, not even in Hamburg, seen so many ruins as on our drive through Berlin to the Stephenses' flat in Franzesbader Strasse. Mr Stephens explained that more than half of the Berlin houses were in ruins. However, I saw none in the street where they lived on the third floor of a block of flats.

The sight of Mrs Stephens was quite a shock. I had probably expected another Mrs Barnetson, some young and elegant beauty. Actually she was a beauty, mainly in her face and hair. The rest of her gave the impression of a slovenly creature in a mauve dressing gown which she appeared to be wearing every day and all day long. I could not – and still cannot – decide if she may, just may, prove even more interesting than Mrs Barnetson. Her two-months-old baby Nicky was almost permanently suckling at his mother's breast. He was a sweet little creature, Tante Anne would love him, but I think that you, Mamushka, would prefer the little two-and-a-half-year-old screaming monkey called Roger, nicknamed Chimpy. At our arrival he was having a battle of willpower with his nursemaid, who could neither persuade, nor force him into his daily bath and called for Mr Stephens' help, who replied "In a minute", just as any busy man would do. Chimpy went on screaming and running around naked in a rather cold flat. I caught him and sang 'Hoppe, hoppe, Reiter' with him on my knees. He listened so intently to the rhythmic German words that he did not even notice when I 'hopped' him into the bath where he splashed around with delight, making ducklings and toy boats compete in wild movements. Lucy told me that he always had fun whenever anyone had tricked or pushed him into his bath, but, spoilt little English brat that he was, the whole screaming performance would start again when he had to come out. So I was prepared for the worst, but managed to make him jump on to the towel on my lap in the middle of an appropriate story. I think that the Stephens were as impressed with my skills as I was myself.

Chimpy wanted me to read or tell him a bedtime story when he was tucked into bed, but his Daddy told him that I was too tired today (actually I was not) and that I would do it tomorrow. My heart leapt in delight at that prospect. Then Mrs Stephens showed me their guest-room, where I could stay for a night or two until Hannelore, my medical student friend from my time in Vienna, would manage to rent a room for me.

Then Chimpy was asleep and Mr and Mrs Stephens had tea and biscuits and bread-and-honey. Mrs Stephens seems to swear by honey for healthy living, just as you do, Mamushka. Then we had whisky and cigarettes; fruit juice only for Mrs Stephens who does not drink alcohol while nursing a baby, and nursing she did, almost all day long. Nicky was suckling with pleasure.

After Daddy had finished the bedtime story, he laid the table for our dinner, all very properly, but not with the same attention to civilized detail as at the Barnetsons' house. We had fish and tinned vegetables and again a desert (I am getting used to regular deserts) of a chocolate pudding. Then, again a bath and bed.

Wednesday night

I am sorry I have not posted this letter before. So much is happening, all so good and exciting. I really like Mrs Stephens now, and more so every day. She is quite different from Mrs Barnetson, in fact, she does not seem English at all to me. She does not use lipstick except for very special occasions. Her dresses are flowing rather than neat and smart when they go out to a party. Often they take me along to parties, museums, concerts, theatres. I find it embarrassing that they always feel they must entertain me when I am sure they would prefer to be by themselves. So, from that point of view it will be good when I move to the room that Hannelore has *found for me, though it is a rather gloomy, cold place. Herr Pohlman took me there and fetched me again for work the following morning.*

Chimpy is my very best friend. He is even more interesting than his parents and he himself is more interested in everything around him than anyone I know. Besides, he is such fun.

Nicky is also fun, more so than most babies. He makes the same lovely cooing noises that most babies make, but his kindly superior way of laughing about us, is quite remarkable, though sometimes it makes me wonder if I have a smudge on my face, or something idiotic.

Now I will try to recount events in chronological order:

On Monday morning I went to see Hannelore, who does not seem to have changed at all since our student days, nearly five years ago. She is now doing an internship at a Berlin hospital, I think it is the Humboldt University hospital, but am not sure. Then Mr Stephens took us on a two-hour sight-seeing tour, wasn't that kind? Afterwards he showed me his (it will be our) very smart office in the Press Club, which he shares with the French journalist Henry de Turenne. Then we walked back to the Stephenses' flat for lunch.

I am not paying for any of this: I would not know how, anyhow. It would embarrass me to offer, except that, of course, I do not accept any wages apart from the money I need for my rent.

In the afternoon we were visited by Monsieur de Turenne. He had just been to Prague, Vienna, Budapest. The very names of those lovely places made my heart beat faster and as it is daily beating fast with excitement, that is saying something! What a life!

In the evening I walked to Hannelore's house to chat and reminisce with her until 9 p.m., then returned to the Stephenses for long talks until 11.30 p.m. Once again I was allowed to have a bath and stay in their guest room.

Next morning we walked to the Press Club, where I skimmed through ever so many Berlin dailies from all four sectors of the city. M. de Turenne was sharing his fantastic chocolates with us in our shared office. That evening we again read papers and shared coffee and chocolates. At 4 p.m. we went back to the flat to give German lessons to Mr Stephens. Unfortunately (for my self-esteem) his German is very good, even better than Tristan's was, so once again I felt pretty useless, but am getting used to being spoilt.

By the way, Tristan sent me a marvellous winter coat from London. He just won't give up wooing me, will he? And you like him?!

On Tuesday night we had a party at the Stephenses' flat. How very different from Military Government parties or those at the News Guardian! Among the guests were Betty Morgan, a cheerful, plump British journalist who appears to have studied art history and French in a number of foreign countries. There were a couple of journalists: the husband had formerly worked in the War Department, now in the CCG; he had studied law, his wife studied art history and music. Frau Winkelmann, Furtwängler's secretary, a member of the aristocracy before her marriage, was telling us about Furtwängler as a person, which was fun, but when the conversation switched to a discussion of music, I was so out of my depth that I sweated with embarrassment.

There was also a German journalist whose wife was an artist and who has lived in Italy from 1943 till now. She wanted to paint me. Not jolly likely, I thought, but was willing to visit her because she was getting invitations to parties with the Soviet cultural attaché and could take me with her: to suckling pigs roasted by the ton, with vodka, which reminded me of Volodya's birthday party. But I would not go without the Stephenses.

In spite of very strong Turkish coffee from cups like those used by the Turkish students in Vienna, we all almost sleep-walked to bed.

A large, long wooden box inlaid with mother-of-pearl patterns is always full of cigarettes which prove too strong a temptation for me. I am smoking one now, while I am writing. The Stephenses are at a reception in the Press Club, where I 'worked' in the morning, gorging myself on the ever-lasting Turenne chocolates.

Friday

I am sure I told you about those strange and wonderful talks I had with Chimpy in my bed in the early mornings, when he seemed to turn the fairy stories I told him into allegories and my philosophies into funny stories... I did not know if to treat him like a toddler or an adult friend. But it was that, more than any other consideration, that made me so happy when the Stephenses asked me to move in with them instead of having those daily trips – and frequent guest-room stays in their flat.

6 November 1947

Thank God, Edith has left with those two awful men! Talking to Edith and Hannelore would have been pleasant, but John and Charles the Bold proved even worse than I remembered them from Hamburg. Praising the initiative of black-marketeers, talking of the need for freedom, meaning that sort of business like any other. Trying to convince us that only businessmen deserved freedom, as they were the only people who knew what to do with freedom, the only ones who, in short, knew how to live. Hence they were spending 1,500 Marks on a meal with the help of our food coupons before driving home between ruins where people searched for bits of coal and such useful items. It all made me feel quite sick. John noticed how I felt, but all that Charles could say was "Is our Anneli beginning to dream of noble principles again? You must learn to live, girl, and this is life." I would rather be dead, but I only thought it without speaking it out aloud. Similar things happened every evening while they were in Berlin and I counted the minutes until I would be back with the Stephenses, where I felt so much at home.

Sometimes I found genuine excuses not to go out with them, such as having to go out with the Stephenses. (I did not have to, but wanted to.)

I remember a wonderful Friday night with the Stewarts, the lovely elderly Scottish couple living on the same floor as we did. Mr Stewart was working for the British Council and was using the council offices for a pianist to play Chopin and Schubert, none of it too highbrow even for me. The other guests were mainly

German lawyers, doctors, actors, musicians, artists, the usual Stewart clientele. The Stephenses and I stayed on for a cup of tea when the other guests had gone.

Nowadays I always get Chimpy ready for nursery school in the morning, after our usual morning-bedtime stories. (Mr Stephens still mostly tells the night-time stories.) My intention was to make it possible for the parents to sleep a little longer, as Nicky often disturbed their nights. But I don't know why, our dressing ritual always turns out a terribly noisy one. I become infected by Chimpy's ideas of fun, turning the effort of pulling a sock over a foot into a wrestling match.

I am always in the Press Club when Chimpy is at school. The latest war of propaganda is really funny, but made me boil with fury when I first read those papers. And the pictures!

It started with a front-page photo in the American-licensed paper 'Der Abend' showing a broadly grinning Stalin next to Ribbentrop. The article below described the Stalin-Hitler alliance. Do you remember, Mamushka, that Tante Anne said at the time that this pact would make the British help the Poles instead of selling them down the drain as they did to the Czechs? In next morning's Tägliche Rundschau (Russian licensed) there was a picture of Chamberlain in the guise of an angel of peace in Munich, the caption saying that Hitler was given license to do what he wanted in the East. Who do they think they are fooling? Or are we really so easily caught by politicians? Sometimes I really wish for anarchy. Well, don't worry, I am not serious, just very angry.

Maybe we will go to Nuremberg soon and I might visit you, but maybe I will just come for Christmas.

13 November 1947

Marlene,
I cannot remember enough of Wallenstein to judge whether Octavio was a goody or a baddy. I would have to read Schiller's entire Wallenstein again... [I waffled on nevertheless on what might have been noble motives behind evil deeds, or not so evil deeds – four entire pages of rubbish, then another two pages about Indian laws being Indian, but made by the British and how the benefits of independence from trade relations with other countries switch from the British master race to American master business.]

Tristan frightens me with soppy love letters. I get claustrophobia at the thought of him, feel quite sick with anger, but try to keep a sense of humour. It's all so absurd: I find Bill much more likeable, but could not possibly marry a man like him and I can't help that awful feeling that I may end up marrying Tristan eventually. If only I could have freedom for a little longer. Why can't men understand that a woman can be totally and happily involved with other things than men? Why should we be itching to look for future chains? Even some women don't understand that; Mrs Stewart is certainly anxious to pair me off with some male. Only the Stephenses understand me. Life with them is certainly the best thing that has ever happened to me. Plus some flirting on the fringe, of course.

We had a marvellous day in the Grunewald. I never knew that there were so many lakes, forests, and hills right inside the city. We left the children behind and, *together with the Stewarts, walked from 10 a.m. till 5 p.m. Mr Stephens carried a rucksack with our lunch picnic. We sat on a bench, a piece of bread in one hand, a piece of cheese in the other, then apples instead of drinks. For our desert we had a small piece of real chocolate, a biscuit and a cigarette.*

Next day we repeated a Grunewald outing, taking Chimpy along to play with Pohlman while we walked for a good hour along the Havel. I realized that the Stephenses are much more athletic than I am, so I resolved to practice high jumps and long jumps, and since I was no longer at school having to do compulsory sports, I rather enjoyed the exercise, not for speed, but to fill my lungs with extra gulps of fresh air. I still think that speed is uncivilized.

Now we have been to the pretty Renaissance Theatre, to see the Heinz Hilper production of 'The Song of the Dove', an American play in German translation. I might write more about it when I have had time to digest. I am extremely slow at understanding plays, perhaps because we had only pre-digested, laundered drama for so many years. Again and again I must pinch myself to believe in my luck of staying with the Stephenses.

After the theatre the Stewarts came in for tea. Now I am writing in bed, long after midnight, almost unable to hold the pen.

I thought it was very unfair that, whenever the Stephenses wanted to invite their friends for a proper dinner after a visit to the theatre, Mrs S. had to stay behind to cook it. On one particular day, the Stewarts wanted to take the Stephenses to the opera and come back for dinner, but Mrs Stephens thought this could not be done because if she started cooking after the opera, her guests would not have a meal before midnight. I rashly said that she could go, because I would cook the dinner. She was delighted, assuming that a young German girl was bound to have had cookery lessons, not knowing that I had been in the academic, not the domestic branch at school. I was determined to try, but my heart sank when I was shown the raw food in the fridge. How stupid spontaneous offers can be! But I did not have the heart to withdraw my offer.

No sooner had Stephenses and Stewarts left the house – the Stewarts live in the same house, on the same floor – than I panicked. I rushed to the telephone, holding the wobbly chunk of meat from the refrigerator, and asked the operator for the Freyersen village phone number. "You do realize that this phone can only be used for official business?" the operator asked. "Of course, this is not a private call, it is a matter of life or death for members of the British press!" I replied boldly, and they consented to connect me.

Herr Brinkmann went to fetch my mother to the phone. She was immediately trying to chat socially in her delighted surprise, but I had to interrupt her and explain my 'business'.

I described the lump of meat as "triangular, wobbly pink, with a bone inside. She guessed it must be something like a leg of lamb and gave detailed descriptions how to roast it, being repeatedly interrupted by the operator insisting that this was private. "Do you want members of the British press and the British Council to starve?" I shouted back. "This is not a private call, but something for an official dinner. You can ask the 'Observer' correspondent." I was reconnected with my mother, who gave me a telephonic cooking lesson for leg of lamb. Unfortunately

51

the Stephenses' cooker did not work in Celsius, but I had never heard of Fahrenheit, so I simply guessed the heat; nor did my mother know what lb. and oz. could stand for on the scales, so I guessed the weight, too. I really did almost as much guessing as if I had not had any instructions: I even guessed the cooking time.

All seemed fairly clear, so I proceeded until I discovered the sprouts. I examined them in horror and again did battle with the operator for the 1-2 minutes required to have my information.

The Stephenses and the Stewarts, came home from the opera to a ready-cooked meal. They enjoyed my cooking except for the sprouts. Mr Stewart said "Lisa is in love", because I had overestimated what my mother described as 'a pinch of salt' and over-salting food is supposed to signify being in love. But they all bravely ate the sprouts without asking for second helpings. What a relief! The Stephens never discovered the preceding drama.

Later I wrote to my mother asking her for simple biscuit recipes, using dry (powdered) eggs in case I wanted to make some quickly for surprise visitors. The few fresh eggs we are sent with our NAAFI-rations – Chimpy calls "The Russians are coming" when these weekly rations arrive – are used boiled for children's breakfasts with bread 'fingers' to dip into the yolks. I wonder if in later years Chimpy will have garbled memories of Russians and rations much in the same way that I remember early arguments between Tante Anne and Onkel Egon.

November, Saturday

Dear Mamushka,
I am planning to go to Dresden on Monday to collect some of the things that are apparently still unbroken at the Hänigs' out-of-town house. Planning is the word. Some jokes give me the creeps. Mr Stephens thinks I should dress up with make-up to make me look very old and to wear shabby, 'proletarian' clothes so that I would be a less likely victim of rape. And to keep the Tägliche Rundschau in my coat pocket, of course. I knew he was not serious, but those are creepy thoughts nevertheless. So I will not post this letter until I have returned. I just have to write some things now in case Dresden later obliterates other events.

We plan to see the film 'Le silence est d'or' tomorrow and next week Musset's 'Andrea del Sarto' in the theatre, possibly in translation. We also intend to see the Russian film 'Colonel Kusmin' in German, which promises to be interesting, possibly awful; I am really looking forward to it and I could thank 'The Observer' on my knees for keeping me here.

Yesterday I went with the Stewarts, without the Stephenses, to an Anglo-German discussion evening at Frau von Kleist's place. I talked mostly to a German doctor whose name I have forgotten, though Mrs Stewart is openly scheming to pair us off, and to a student from the technical college, whose name is Uhrmacher. We discussed concepts of idealism, cynicism, hope.

The Stewarts will invite the Stephenses, that doctor, and me to have dinner with them soon.

Dresden was very interesting. I did dress in an awful raincoat, hair pinned under a scarf, face smudged, paper sticking out of my pocket.

The town is razed to the ground, much worse than Berlin, even worse than Kiel.

Fortunately the Hänigs live away from central Dresden and all our stuff was still there, untouched by Russian soldiers or German thieves. Saxon dialect, Rudi's lukewarm handshakes, his affectionate hugs and adoring eyes get on my nerves, but I was bearing it with truly heroic patience. Poor man, he can't help his boring goodness that borders on saintliness. How could he understand that most girls prefer rogues?

Needless to say, I had no chance to admire Dresden's famous art and architecture, but walking between the ruins was interesting and less exhausting than doing the same had been with Rita and Tristan in Hamburg. Here, at least, the sun was not blazing relentlessly on my gin-aching head. The Hänigs, being almost teetotallers, would not have understood my gin story.

I carried as much as I could and gave up the proletarian look for the return journey. Rudi said that he would bring us the rest, heaven help me. Väti was his father-substitute and now he is piling the force of his love for my father on top of his peculiar love for me. But I will have to let him come. I took mocca cups, crystal plates, a very thin bone china Chinese tea set, crystal glasses and your precious large blue engagement vase. All that was quite heavy enough without adding bed and table linen and clothes except for those I was wearing. But when, after all my trouble getting and carrying our property, Mr Stephens stated calmly that property corrupts, I felt quite angry.

December 1947

Months later people teased Bob that Taqui had pulled a fast one on him and pinched his secretary for her own mother's help, a job I felt much more qualified for, anyhow. But while Chimpy was at nursery school I still went most mornings to the press club to justify the salary that The Observer was paying me and which I did not want at all, because everything I wanted was free. I often took a spoonful of condensed milk out of a tin which I loved since the American prisoners-of-war had thrown us such a tin in return for freshly baked bread in Mecklenburg in March 1945.

Most of the journalists in the press club, all working for British newspapers or Reuters, were interesting to talk to and to have drinks with, particularly when Mrs Stephens dropped in to fetch us for lunch. Occasionally I worked in the office in the afternoon, but I spent most afternoons doing things with Chimpy and sometimes also with Mrs Stephens, if she found a baby-sitter for Nicky and if she did not have more interesting things to do. At other times, particularly in good toboganing or ice-skating weather, I did not go to the press club at all. In the evenings we had guests, or took turns going out, either the Stephenses or I. People made a habit of theatre visits followed by dinner at home. Sometimes I cooked the dinner, occasionally I had to battle with the operator when I wanted my mother's help, but generally my cooking only went wrong when baby Nicky decided to yell in the middle of my concentration. He was sweet as babies go, but he could not articulate his wishes properly.

Mr and Mrs Stephens took the baby with them when they went to London for about ten days, but thought it was pointless to drag Chimpy along on such a strenuous journey. I was extremely happy to be left in charge of my best friend and enjoyed every minute of the days we had just to play, to tell stories and to eat baked beans, followed by condensed milk. I did not mind that Chimpy had a cough, because I knew from my own childhood that this could easily be cured by sucking sugar-lumps dipped in rum. But when, very early one morning, Chimpy woke me with loud shouts of "Lisa (that was what the Stephens called me), I need rum!" in a voice that could be heard all through the house, I nearly fainted before I rushed to oblige him. What would the Stewarts think of me, and of the Stephenses for leaving a two and a half-year-old toddler in charge of an enemy girl? Many people had thought the Stephenses mad to leave Chimpy even before they left; even more so did the people in Britain, who imagined Berlin to be a dangerous place. For the rest of that week I noticed looks of distrust whenever we met someone on the stairs, but I must have imagined them. Nobody actually said anything.

But one day I began to distrust myself – I just could not find Chimpy anywhere in the flat. Then I noticed that the door was slightly ajar. I ran along the street calling "Chimpy!" and then saw him, walking briskly along the pavement.

"What on earth do you think you are doing?"

"I am going to get a bus to London", he replied.

"But I thought you were happy to stay with me."

"I am", he said, "I only want to see Mummy and Daddy for a minute."

"You can't do that. London is a long way off and you would need an aeroplane."

"That will be lovely, I like planes."

I convinced him that he would be happier coming back with me.

We baked *Marmorkuchen*, licked the mixing bowl together, went to the press club together, where Chimpy could play safely with a scooter, and with various dogs belonging to journalists. He was very funny with dogs, at times really rough, flexing his muscles; then again affectionate, cuddling them, and then again for no reason I could find, suddenly very scared of them. Maybe he was always scared and only bolstered his courage with boxing and cuddling in turn.

When Pohlman took us shopping, it really required two people to watch Chimpy, who always loved exploring and often managed to disappear. Of course, I had learnt to watch out after the recent escape experience.

Most times he was happy, but when the other Stephenses came back, I was the one most overjoyed about having a complete family again.

Every now and then Bob took me to West Germany. He taught me to play chess on a travelling set in the back of the car. As he did not really need me in the American Press Club in Frankfurt, I often accepted offers of lifts to Hamburg and hence to Freyersen. Hamburg papers were run by members of the British control commission who came to Frankfurt for briefings.

The Observer correspondent for Russia, Edward Crankshaw, came to stay with us. He told us that no-one could feel indifferent about Russia – they either hated the country or fell in love with it. He belonged to Russia's lovers, not for her politics, but for the people, the music, the poetry. I loved it all – not the man, who was long married and not the falling-in-love type. But he was a flirt, just like myself!

He took me to see a wonderful film, 'Les enfants du paradis', and while watching Marcel Marceau, Crankshaw stroked and squeezed my hand. He could not see in the dark that I nearly collapsed with laughter. I did not really want him to see, because I liked it. It was flattering to receive attentions from a man like him.

All of us, the Stephenses, Crankshaw and myself spent more time exploring Berlin and the Grunewald than in the office. In the evening we read the papers at home, where we could all discuss them together. And so the bombshell of Marshal Sokolovsky's speech at the Control Commission dropped right into our flat.[6]

Scooped by the SED (Socialist Unity Party)

There had been an agreement between the Allies to withhold publication until next day, by which time the speech could have been translated precisely for all papers to use. The Western-licensed papers kept to that agreement, but the SED papers made that speech the morning's scoop for all of them, complete with suitable commentaries, of course. There was very little that the Western papers could do in their evening papers and on the following morning to limit the damage. Everyone in the press club worked in frenzied fury and General Clay called a press conference. Meanwhile I enjoyed the Grunewald with Mrs Stephens and their children, without the men.

They had begun to call me 'Lisa', as Chimpy had done from the time we first met. I thought this was a kind, friendly way to address me, though I actually disliked the name. Sometimes they seemed to hint that they would like me to call them by their Christian names, answering the phone with "Bob speaking", or

---

[6] As reported by AP (on 23 November 1947): "BERLIN, Nov. 22. — Soviet Marshal Vassily D. Sokolovsky denounced the western Allies' occupation policies in Germany in a 10,000-word attack published today [...] Although there was an understanding that a four-power communiqué reporting on yesterday's Control Council meeting would be issued jointly at noon today, the Russians published Marshal Sokolovsky's charges in full in their morning newspapers in Berlin. The official Russian news agency had the accusations in print for German readers while the press relations officers of the western powers still were working on translations of the communiqué and arranging press briefings to give the Allied side of the story."

"Taqui speaking", but I did not have the guts to accepts such familiar terms just then.

Mrs Stewart seemed to have another hope to pair me off, and the man was either in league with her or enjoyed the idea without prompting. I found it difficult not to giggle when he tried so hard. His name was something like Leube. He was a sculptor and a friend of Kolbe's. We all tinkled on the Stewarts' piano and sang a potpourri of German folk, student and Christmas songs. I could never sing in tune, but didn't care, as long as the others sang louder.

Chimpy could now sing "Alle meine Entchen" and "Hoppe, hoppe, Reiter" accompanied by the right actions.

We saw the film 'Colonel Kusmin' at last, a really good propaganda piece, claiming all the noble virtues for Russian people and their army, rather like Nazi films had done. Even now there were many Germans who believed in such noble aspects of their own people and called everything else that had happened "just a few aberrations".

Sometimes, in the evening, Mr Stephens read Goethe's *Faust* with me while his wife made our supper, after which we all read Virginia Woolf.

Letters from Freyersen were beginning to take a long time, but Mr Stephens reassured my mother that if anything went wrong, they would phone the Brinkmanns straight away.

After my Christmas visit to Freyersen – the usual, beautiful kind of Christmas with a large tree and real candles – I reached Hanover at 4 a.m. and travelled by train via Helmstedt to Berlin, reaching the Stephenses' flat at 11 a.m., which was surprisingly quick. I went out with Chimpy on his new scooter. He was excited about his Christmas present and could ride it quite well.

In the evening the Lynkers came, bringing presents for all of us – my own being a lovely Norwegian book in German translation. The Lynkers were interested in the origins of words and in very ancient history, going back 3,000 to 4,000 years. They were talking about pre-Egyptian culture in the Sahara and Indian toilets at the same period. It made me wonder whether one day, after an atomic war, someone might dig up our present civilisation and say: "How fantastic, they appear to have known how to build cars!" But I was relieved when the conversation turned to more recent times and whether the Trojan Wars were fiction or fact. At least I could participate in that conversation.

We went to a press conference with Kaiser, who was not a patch on Schumacher. I was fed up with all these excuses and lies and would have welcomed anarchy. I constantly had to remind myself of the motto I had hanging over my desk at home, 'Carpe diem' – seize the day. Every day was well worth taking as it came.

I saw 'Octoberman' with Mrs Stephens. It was good.

Unbelievably, I beat Mr Stephens at chess; whereupon he wanted his revenge, and we completely forgot that the chauffeur Pohlman was sitting outside our house, waiting in the car in the freezing cold. He should have rung the bell, I thought. In the end I just went with him to pick up the papers and collect a parcel for the Stephenses from the customs office.

On my return I found a beautifully laid tea table with lace mats made of silver paper under crystal plates, candles, crackers at everyone's place, fruitcake with marzipan and biscuits. As Chimpy could not sleep, we wrapped him in a blanket to join us for dinner a little later.

The Schumachers came to join us for this New Year's Eve celebration. They were Germans who had emigrated to the U.S.A. and were now working – really working compared with most – for the CCG. They told me that after all these years they were still counting in German for numbers above twenty.

Chimpy realized that we were boring in the evening and wanted to go to bed after the soup. He then slept till 8 a.m. next morning, which was marvellous. We finished a meat course, then tinned peaches and custard. We drank white German wine.

Conversation with the Schumachers was not as exciting as with the Stewarts, or Betty Morgan, or the AFP correspondent de Turenne and his beautiful Texan girlfriend Lynn, or the Mendelssohns, but it was all right to talk about differences between German and British customs, about Berlin orphanages, about the way Americans pronounce English. We had coffee and cake and listened to Beethoven and Tchaikovsky on the radio we had borrowed for the night, waiting, with a filled wine glass next to us, "… only 30 seconds… only ten seconds… only one second till 1948", and then we toasted each other with "Happy New Year." We went to our balcony to hear the church bells ringing and see the fireworks.

In the morning, when Mrs Stephens woke up, she noticed to her horror and amusement that a man had overdone the New Year's Eve celebrations. There he was, still in his dinner jacket and wearing a top hat, climbing along the rooftop opposite. She did not realize that chimney sweeps did such antics to bring good luck to people on New Year's Day.

Meanwhile Claus had decided to sign on as a civilian labourer in Scotland. Our mother was worried when he wrote he intended to send her a parcel. I re-assured her that he would not do this unless he could afford it, and that she should really ask for a pair of shoes for Marlene if he had coupons to spare. Marlene really needed shoes and there was no need for a mother to feel embarrassed about accepting presents from her own son.

I was trying to buy as many books as possible in the Russian zone, where such items were cheap. If Mamushka could start a small, private lending library, she could have a little extra income, even if she did not charge much. So many refugees had now moved out of farmers' houses into rooms of their own where they had little else to do but read. Unlike the almost illiterate farmers, they wanted to read, but really had no money for the library, unless her lending prices were very low. So she charged only 5 Pfennigs per book per week.

In Freyersen I heard that Usch's fiancé had abandoned her since she was no longer likely to inherit much. What a swine! But we also heard some good news via Dr Maas, formerly administrator of the Beynuhnen estate in East Prussia and a close friend of the Honskamps. He wrote that the widower had married his sister-in-law, whom I expected to become a much better wife than Gisela's mother had been. The latter had been mostly her two children's mother, rather than her husband's wife. I had always liked Gisela's aunt. Her brother Jürgen, a soldier, had been killed.

Hannelore thought that the black market was a good means for students to support their parents and that it actually prevented crime. But it was frightening to contemplate the effects of a currency reform, particularly in Berlin.

I nearly exploded with anger when The Observer front page had an article (maybe by the Reuters Berlin correspondent, certainly not by Bob Stephens) reporting that 'a Russian shot an American soldier in the American sector of Berlin.' What had in fact happened was this: at one of the big parties in the American sector everybody had had much too much whisky. One of these drunkards, a Russian soldier, walked into the street with his loaded pistol and tried some target shooting at the first lit-up figure he saw. It was awful, of course, but not political. Just a week before, I had felt annoyed at the aggressive, provocative tone of a speech Churchill had made.

When I had my regular health check-up, the doctor and nurses were envious about the way I retained my summer tan on my back and midriff, but I was glad we had real winter now.

Chimpy and I built a marvellous snowman, after which we decided to borrow ice skates from the Schneider family. Evi, Lori's young sister, was thrilled with the fact that such a little boy could speak real English, which was a difficult subject for her at school. Chimpy found her admiration embarrassing, but was also amused in a superior sort of way. He loved the Schneiders' black rabbit and could hardly be persuaded to leave it. But Evi's doll puzzled him – so big and life-like, similar to Nicky with eyes that opened and closed. "But she does not talk to me," he said in a sad voice. We borrowed three pairs of skates of the right size for Mr Stephens, Pohlman and either Mrs or myself, as we had the same size feet.

When we were leaving, Chimpy was determined to open the car door himself. Though he struggled for some time and made Evi laugh, he managed and then tried to hold it open for me to climb in first. At this Evi collapsed with laughter. Chimpy found this so puzzling that on our return journey he asked again and again "Why did that girl laugh?" and began to giggle himself at the thought.

The Stephenses were nice to Lori, the daughter of my mother's finishing-school friend. Mr Stephens visited them on his own once, when he was in the Russian sector. When Lori came to visit me one Sunday, we were offered real coffee and bread with butter and marmalade.

Lori told me about two good-looking Russians she had met, one of them from Leningrad. They both squeezed as much information as they could out of her, her family, schooling, present work, but she learnt almost nothing about them, only about the difference between the international, or 'evangelical' Red Cross and the Russian Red Cross. It made the evangelical group sound prejudiced as to who deserved help.

We went on walking and had a snack lunch in a restaurant near the Kurfürstendamm, using my coupons, as I wanted to give the Stephenses a day off from me.

The Stephenses' lunch visitors that day were the Lufts. Frau Luft painted, but I did not really like her paintings. She seemed fascinated by ruins and somehow made them look like romantic photographs.

When I came back with Lori, Mrs Stephens had baked a kind of rolls which she called scones, especially for us. She did not want any tea, because they had had a late lunch. We ate in my room. Chimpy kept on saying that it was cosy. He was sweet to Lori, and she found it difficult to part from him. But she had to be at her home quite early.

Mrs Stephens and I then went to the cinema to see the French version of 'Crime and Punishment', a very good film. It made me think, though, that compared with all the horror of their past history, the present dictatorship must seem almost pleasant to the Russian people.

The most exciting cultural event in Berlin was the French import of the première of 'Les Mouches' in the presence of Jean-Paul Sartre himself, in whose honour the French embassy gave a cocktail party. Mr Stephens allowed me to go to the party on behalf of 'The Observer', not because he was not interested, but because he knew of my infatuation with existentialism, especially Sartre and Camus.

Sartre struck me as a little, respectable-looking man, modest, almost shy. He preferred to talk about Berlin rather than his own works. I liked the party, but the performance of 'Les Mouches' next day was even more wonderful. My skin prickled with goose-flesh and I was afraid to lose even a single word of the masterpiece. Mr Stephens and M. de Turenne offered to find as many Sartre and Camus works as they could for me.

Another event, not as stimulating but exciting nevertheless, was the première of the opera 'Manon' at the state opera house. Mr Buschmann[7], the Prussian-looking ladykiller who lived at the edge of a Grunewald Lake where he had a sailing boat, invited us to the opera and introduced us to Messrs. Piek and Grotewohl (presidents of the newly created East German Republic), also to Dr Friedensburg and Dr Acker (successive mayors of the city), and several Russian generals whose names I cannot remember. After the performance some of those who came from the British sector joined us for coffee at the Stephenses' flat, which was now in Hohenzollerndamm.

In the same week I saw 'Film without Title', also 'Something in the Wind' in the NAAFI cinema. Mrs Stephens took me to the Kolbe exhibition 'Night over Germany'. One day I went to the House of Soviet Culture with Lori, to see a film about Moscow. When we came out to go to the underground station Friedrichstraße, we found ourselves in the middle of a rather scary roundup.

Some worrying things were going on which I did not understand: Mr Stephens thought he might have to go to Bavaria to some secret conference. I knew that soon, somewhere, new German laws and a proper German constitution would have to be worked out. Recently a train had been stopped at Marienborn[8], and people had begun to talk of war. Then the talk and the fears died again. But I knew that planning for that eventuality was continuing.

---

[7] Possibly Hugo Buschmann (1899-1983), journalist, economist and politician.

[8] Checkpoint Alpha (the main crossing between West and East Germany, although it was not called a 'border' as the Allies refused to recognize East Germany until 1973) lay between Helmstedt and Marienborn. Numerous incidents occurred there, particularly trains being held up due to disputes over the Russian right to inspect Allied trains or the need for all documentation to have Russian translations.

Mr Stephens told me that they hoped to obtain a visitor's visa for me to go with them on a visit to England, to meet some of their friends and relatives. A wonderful thought, but why just now? Mrs Stephens said that they would be sad if at some time in the future I would live far away from them. Perhaps they could find me a job in London, where I could visit them every day or, better still, receive permission to – nominally – employ me as their mother's help. Why nominally? Surely they knew that I could not dream of a better life than looking after Chimpy and Nicky? It would be perfect until Chimpy – by then probably called Roger – went to school.

The Observer asked me to write obituaries of famous people, so that they could keep them in readiness for their possible deaths. My first subject was to be Pastor Niemöller. I was pleased to delve into the life of such a man. In this connection I went to see Frau von Arnheim, a nice woman, living in a lovely flat. She was really much too nice. She went out of her way to be kind and I felt trapped by her friendliness, as if we were to be inseparable for life. Perhaps she assumed that I was a good Christian, or maybe she wanted to turn me into one. Her biscuits tasted like the bread at communion after my confirmation. Perhaps it was not the taste but the way she talked that reminded me of confirmation and communion. Yet I liked her and did not want to hurt her feelings. So I agreed rather half-heartedly to visit her again.

More letters to my mother

30 January 1948

Mamushka, can you believe the news? Surely it must be some terrible mistake, perhaps by a Reuters reporter. But I can't stop crying... and nor can Mrs Stephens. Gandhi, the great man of peace, the wonderful man who abhorred all violence now himself a victim to violence? It just can't have happened. Who would do such a thing? I must put it on paper, IT IS NOT TRUE!, so that I can sleep at night. Perhaps there will be different news in the morning.

How can it be true? There were people like Hitler, who 'miraculously' survived assassination attempts again and again with the luck of the Devil and called it 'protected by providence' – and now a man like Gandhi, the epitome of non-violence?

Next morning:

It is true, they say. Everything suddenly looks so pointless. And Hannelore wants me to get a costume ready for a masked ball with medical students... and Rudi from Dresden wants me to do the same for a grand opera ball! Shit! I won't post this letter until I have filled the envelope to the postage stamp's worth. But at the moment there is nothing to say.

Friday 13 – but I am not superstitious, I think.

And, à la Sartre (or should one say 'au Sartre'?) I have decided that there is no point in moping and despair, not even about Gandhi, and every point in activity. I don't think Sartre had my kind of activities in mind. When you read my letters, you will wonder if I ever do any work at all. I wonder myself.

The medical students' masked ball was actually quite a stiff, conventional affair, not the frivolous fun I had expected.

I include programmes of the latest cinema & theatre outings instead of my own comments. You will understand that I enjoy things, unless I comment to the contrary. Read programme notes on 'The Abyss within Herr Gerstenberger' and the 'Magic Flute', which I saw with Mrs Stephens, Mrs Stewart, and Lori while Hannelore did the baby-sitting for the two children she loves. The absence of taxis after the performance was really awful for Mrs Stewart.

As you can see, Gorki's 'My Universities' was in Russian and made me feel ever so homesick for Vitya, Volodya, Dyeda, Katya, Galya… even for those months spent on the road and in sheds. Silly, really, when I so much enjoy all the luxuries here, including lovely, hot baths. When I told the Stephens about my silly nostalgia we talked quite a lot about those days in open carriages and snow and they both urged me to write it all down. But there is no time, there is too much living to do, remembering the past seems such a waste of time.

As it is, I often read in bed till 2 a.m., even till 3 sometimes, and still I can't manage the few books I want to read. I am not a fast reader.

At the 'Traviata' performance many of the Russian audience were wearing enormously long riding boots, also for 'Il Seraglio'.

When I saw 'Nicholas Nickleby' I had again the same impression of life in England that we were given at school, only now I know that this kind of socially cruel England no longer exists. Perhaps I will find out more soon, but not too soon, I hope.

Most of my 'Observer' work now means research into the lives of famous men, but Chimpy becomes furious when I do any writing at all after he has come back from school. So I try to leave things until he is in bed, and then it is so tempting to talk to the Stephenses or their visitors. No day is long enough.

At the SED offices they always treat me as if I were a spy. Theirs is quite the most horrible, gloomy, unfriendly place in the whole of Berlin.

Of course I agree with the idea of recycling papers, but the postage for sending them to Marlene would be higher than the eventual proceeds.

How I would love to advise Marlene on patterns for her dresses and how I look forward to seeing those materials! I had a very happy phone-call from Tristan yesterday, telling me that his salary had gone up from 800 pounds to 1,000 and how well WE (!) could live on that. And Bill keeps writing, not soppy love letters, but urging me to give him an honest answer as to why I don't want to marry him. He cannot understand – hardly anyone can – that I quite simply do not want to get married, full stop. He seems to think that I either already have found, or am waiting for a Mr Right, when I am not waiting for anything of the sort. What is the point of replying, when it is like talking to a wall? I will just stop writing, I think.

Tomorrow Lori and I will go to 'Kabale und Bühne' (Vaudeville in the House of Soviet Culture) and on Sunday we have tickets for a Furtwängler concert.

And now I am going to bed.

15 February 1948

Dear Mamushka,

Again I find myself too short of time to write a proper letter, so I will just write a few words, or maybe sentences every day.

Yesterday we went to hear Furtwängler conduct and had super pea soup and cakes at the Schneiders. I am so glad it began to snow again. It is quite beyond me how anyone actually likes living in a hot country. We have so much fun skiing in the Grunewald and ice-skating on different lakes. Once I even managed to dance on skates with Pohlman.

16 February 1948

In the morning I walked to the Mendelssohns with Mrs Stephens. Mrs Mendelssohn writes books under her maiden name, Hilde Spiel. They are both Jewish refugees from Austria. In the afternoon I went tobogganing with Chimpy and was talking to him in German, which he understands fairly well.

17 February 1948

I went to a press conference on education, which was fairly interesting, though it was not clear what they intended to do.

18 Feb.

Marvellous, invigorating walk in the Grunewald in wonderful wind and snow.

19 February 1948

A day like most others. Evening guests were a friend of Betty Morgan and Hannelore.

20 February 1948

Mrs Stewart's birthday party was as good as all their parties, full of folk songs from different countries. Met a nice Dr Linden and Sievers.

21 February 1948

An interesting man, the writer Wolfgang Hildesheimer came to stay with us. He spent all morning going round most of the bookshops with the Stephenses while I enjoyed Chimpy. In the evening Mrs Stephens went out while I made supper for Mr Stephens and Hildesheimer and we talked into the early morning hours.

22 February 1948

We had breakfast with Mr Hildesheimer, then the Mendelssohns and Lufts came to visit. In the afternoon I took Chimpy on his toboggan to the Mendelssohns. Sybille was here. In the evening M. de Turenne and Lynn came again.

23 February 1948

During morning skiing with Mrs Stephens I nearly collapsed with laughter. Then she went to bed and I played with Chimpy in the snow Alas! We had locked ourselves out and had to wait for Herr Lehman to help with a pick-lock. Later that evening the Stephens went to a party in evening dress. Mrs S. looked stunning in a long white gown. Hildesheimer returned to the flat at 10 p.m. and presented me with a Büchner book. We talked till 2 a.m., by which time the Stephenses had returned. "Mrs Stephens, you are drunk again," I greeted her. Well, as you might notice, every day is full of similar occupations like skiing, skating, building snowmen, tobogganing, just walking; and every evening we have different visitors, some spending the night with us, others only the day.

Occasionally I actually work for The Observer, such as trying to write about farmers and farming problems.

Someone called Anthony enquired after Chimpy again and again; he must like him very much. Once we ate our picnic sandwiches standing on skis while Chimpy was playing his own games in the snow.

But the sun is getting stronger and is shining for longer. Spring is in the air and we think we can prepare a party in the garden for Chimpy, the press club garden, of course. Even our rather grand flat in Hohenzollerndamm has no garden.

Chimpy, Anthony, Patricia and I later walked along the Havel, exploring deep holes. The adults had a maddeningly long wait for their plane. They were going to the West, to visit Clarita von Trott, the murdered Adam's widow and her children. Lori came to spend the night with me. Evi also came, finding our life very luxurious. Children played silly games: "I have a dolly", "I have a ducky", which went on and on. Patricia and Chimpy are sweet together, feeling important, as Chimpy is three years old now.

In the evening Gretel Schneider and all her children came to stay with me. I was 'teaching' Eberhard chess. We had a cosy late breakfast next morning. Later I met Lori and Evi again when I was taking Chimpy, Patricia, and a picnic bag to the Havel. Children's conversation can be ever so hilarious; it was hard to remain serious.

Later, when Pohlman and I took Lori and Evi home, an American officer caused a terrible fuss for us in the middle of the street, shouting very annoying American versus British rubbish. It was early in the day, but he already seemed drunk.

On Marlene's birthday (8 March) I tried to phone her at the Dregers, then at Edith's place, but was not successful. Then I fetched the papers, wrote to the Stephenses and cooked potato soup for supper with Peter, Pohlman, Anthony and Graham Smith. I expressed concern with 'hunger-children', but no longer remember what I meant.

The following morning Sybille walked with us along the Havel to the Kaiser-Wilhelm-Turm. The fir branches in the forest are ever so beautiful, and so was our macaroni-cheese supper.

The following days were cooler again and we saw ice crystals on our walk as far as the South End club and around the peninsula. Chimpy and I were singing loudly. We watched fishermen. Then Chimpy tripped and cried. He had not done that since the day when he had a fist fight with Patricia, which was stopped by an American soldier.

From then on we had the usual, unusual series of actions and visitors. Chimpy was pleasantly excited when Gretel Schneider came to baby-sit while the rest of us went out to a party.

In Weertzen / Freyersen the public phone seems to have changed to Werner Jöllenbek. I shall often phone you, Mamushka, though I know this is a much longer way for you to come to the phone than it was at the Brinkmanns. In any circumstances, don't panic, Mamushka.

Spring

I had to phone Dr Linden, because Chimpy had spots and the school asked me to fetch him before lunch. He said it was only chickenpox, not scarlet fever, as I had feared, thinking of my Vitya. He slept in my bed that night, while his parents returned from the West. The weather had cooled, and I liked to feel his feverish body next to mine.

Mr Stephens came to Freyersen with me. It was the first time he had met Mamushka, and he promised to bring his wife with him next time.

We heard that Sokolovsky had walked out of the Control Council[9], which caused consternation everywhere. I thought "Better red than dead" and carried on with my normal life.

It was real spring now and I listened to the birds singing in the Grunewald, wishing that spring would spread all around and last forever.

Lori and I spent a day in Sanssouci – no longer adorned in air-raid camouflage – and met a lovely, middle-aged married Russian couple. The CCG and Sokolovsky seemed distant and unreal, whilst Vitya and Volodya seemed close at the sound of this couple's voices. My whole body contracted when I thought of Vitya. And yet, there was sunshine in Sanssouci and, in keeping with the name of the place, I could not allow melancholy to overcome me.

The Stephens and I now borrowed bicycles instead of skis or skates. Pohlman followed us by car with Chimpy and his scooter inside. I pretended to race the car and Chimpy screamed with delight. It was a wonderful day.

So was our afternoon with the Schneiders in Weissensee Park. People enjoyed the peaceful evening, sipping lemonade on the terraces, boating, Russian soldiers playing ball games on the grass like young boys. Again I felt that nostalgic pain,

---

[9] 20 March 1948: the Soviet Union saw proposals for currency reform as undermining the four-power control of Germany agreed at Potsdam. The Control Council could no longer function, and the Cold War soon ensued.

which seemed unfair to Chimpy, whom I also loved. How many people can one love at the same time? Can it be wrong when married adults have love affairs? Why should anyone ever promise to love one person and only one? What about their children?

There was a Russian film called 'The Man with the Gun', about a man standing there to protect, not frighten people.

Dark Clouds in Berlin

The Observer people – mainly Tristan – were doing their damnedest to make us leave Berlin. They sent a telegram to General Robertson, asking if the family of their correspondent and their secretary should leave Berlin at once. Robertson cabled only one word in reply: 'Rubbish'. I hoped they blushed, but I feared that Tristan had no sense of shame. He kept on phoning and phoning, not accepting even Robertson's judgement. How could he imagine that I of all people should ever marry a panicky man like him?

As Mr Stephens has gone to Finland, where, much to my envy, he was going to visit Sibelius in his Karelian home, and as this was 'a period of high tension' in Berlin, The Observer sent its music correspondent, Charles Reid, to do the reporting in Stephens' place. He was an ever-frantic reporter, working like a madman, day and night... ah, well, I was not sure how much actual work he did at night in the Press Club. Sometimes, coming home between 3 and 4 a.m., he rang the doorbell loudly, although he had a key to the flat for which he fumbled unsuccessfully. Then, leaning against the wall, he groaned: "Aspirin, please, Miss Wiemer!" The first time he did this, I had to wake Mrs Stephens, but then I began to keep aspirins in my room, safely out of Chimpy's reach. He wrote for hours on end, so maybe all his drinking was a way of finding out about Berlin. He was blissfully, annoyingly ignorant of the city.

As Mr Reid spoke no German, I now had little time for Chimpy. Reid pumped me for information about which of the new German political parties stood for what. Dr Pünder from the CDU might have been better equipped to give such information, but I could not get hold of him.

In addition to working directly with Reid, The Observer had asked me to write an obituary for Dr Schumacher. I still could not get used to the idea that, as soon as they heard that a politician was in hospital, they buried him, but I enjoyed finding the details of Schumacher's life.

I also had to translate most of the German papers from beginning to end, not choosing what to translate from the headlines. It took ages and was rather tedious. Thank heaven papers did not have advertisements in those days!

At night Reid stayed on in the club while I went home. Mrs Stephens went to the cinema, Mrs Mendelssohn came to visit me. She and I spent hours reminiscing about Vienna, where she had lived until 1936. She left at 2 a.m., an hour before Reid returned. Mrs Stephens had long gone to bed. Mr Reid had ordered Pohlman to come at 6 a.m. He could easily manage on 2-3 hours' sleep, that short, but tough little man.

Pohlman took us to Charlottenburg station to interview people in the streets. In the Press Club people had been telling stories about two trains being held up at Marienborn and passengers producing picnics while they had to wait. It is hilarious when trains are held up for absurd reasons and for absurdly long periods. I rather enjoyed the crazy situation.

At first I found it extremely embarrassing to do the Reid-style interviews of people in the street. He did ask most peculiar questions. In the Lustgarten, where some fairground people were cleaning up their merry-go-rounds and swings, he asked: "Do Russian people come to the fair? – Do they go on roundabouts? Do they laugh? How do they laugh?" At that last question I blushed and explained to the fairground people that it was not I who asked these questions, but the strange British reporter. I blushed when reading any of Mr Reid's reports. They were so different from Mr Stephens' writing, quite pointless, I thought. But Tristan said on the phone that the reports were marvellously lively, 'giving a very real picture of Berlin.' I wondered if even Mr Stephens might approve of them in some way. He once told us that one should read The News of the World to understand how real people live and think.

Apart from four trains standing around at Marienborn station, there were 'incidents' at Gatow airfield and at the management office of the Reichsbahn in Anhalter station.[10]

We were told on the phone – by Tristan, of course – that the Observer was recalling Stephens from Finland, so that he would be here to help, if we had to move to Frankfurt in a hurry. At least he said "if", not "when", but I was boiling with fury. This was the fourth call from London that day. They must have gone mad, I thought.

I phoned the Warners, or rather Mrs Stephens, who was visiting them now, mainly to let off steam. They all agreed with me, and Mrs Stephens stated categorically that she would refuse to obey Tristan, who was obviously behind all these evacuation plans. He was wetting his pants with fear on our account, I thought.

Tristan's secret letters

After my mother's death I discovered two letters Tristan had written to her, saying that I should not read them. I copy them here.

Letter No 1, dated 3 April (1948):

My dear Mutti,
Very many thanks for your letter of March 26, which reached me today.

---

[10] A Soviet fighter collided with a British/American airliner above Gatow on 5 April 1948, killing all on board. The Reichsbahn office was the headquarters for the Soviet transport department, who were responsible for all railways within Berlin, and was guarded by Red Army soldiers. However, it was located inside the American zone, and in April 1948 it was seized by American soldiers.

I am going to talk to you first about Berlin. Anneli will be very angry with me for doing so, because she thinks that you may worry unnecessarily. She has asked me not to talk to you about Berlin. But I feel it is my duty to tell you what is happening – so I will disobey her "order". I think you will worry less if you know the facts than if you do not know them. (But if you want to save me from Anneli's anger, then perhaps you will not tell her about this letter!)

The first thing to tell you is that everyone here at the Observer believes that there is NOT going to be a war about Berlin. The Russians are expected to go just as far as they dare – without a war. It is quite true that they can make the position of the Allies in Berlin very uncomfortable. But no-one here believes that the Russians will start shooting. They will probably do everything possible to make people think that they are ready to start – but (we believe) they will not shoot.

The second thing is that we are all watching the Berlin situation very carefully and we have the safety of Mrs Stephens and the children and Anneli in the front of our thoughts. You can be quite certain that we intend to do everything possible to look after them. And we are giving special attention to the position of Anneli as a German insofar that might affect her leaving Berlin.

Thirdly, we have advised Stephens to return to Berlin from Finland and we have advised him also to arrange for the movement of his family from Berlin to the British Zone (Anneli included of course). We have done this simply as a safety precaution, because we do not see that anything is gained by keeping them there.

Fourthly, we are trying to arrange for temporary accommodation for the family and Anneli to be provided in Düsseldorf, until accommodation is ready for them in Frankfurt. This would mean that Stephens could work in Frankfurt (which is a better centre than Düsseldorf), but would be within easy distance of his family.

Fifthly, Berlin is not cut off from the West. At the time of writing this letter, British buses are moving freely along the autobahn to Helmstedt and over the zonal frontier into the British zone.

Sixthly: Charles Reid, our temporary correspondent in Berlin, is living in the Stephenses' flat and he is thoroughly reliable and sensible. I spoke to him on the phone today (as I have almost every day this week) and he says they are all very cheerful.

But he also says that Anneli is strongly opposed to leaving Berlin. I knew this already of course. She can be very obstinate sometimes – and at times when obstinacy does not help the situation. Probably she thinks that I am "interfering", but this decision to move them from Berlin is not my decision at all. It is the decision of the Editor of the paper, which he has taken after consultation with all the people here who should know. (Needless to say, I agree with it). It does not seem to occur to Anneli that we probably know a great deal more about the situation in Berlin than she does, even though we are in London. So I think it might be a good idea if you were to write to her (without mentioning this letter or any of the facts in it) that you would personally feel much happier if she was to leave Berlin. She will probably be more ready to listen to you than to us. We are not moving them because we think they are in danger; we are doing it simply because it is silly to take unnecessary risks.

That is all I can tell you. I hope it is enough to show you that we are taking good care of her and that there really is no need to worry. If you feel I could tell you anything else that you need to know, the best thing is to get some officer (English) in Zeven to send me a telegram: ("Jones Observer London, please ring Freyersen" is enough) and I will telephone you. But, honestly, there is no cause for worry.

I spoke to Stephens on the phone today in Helsinki and he is not in the least bit worried. In fact he was very reluctant to return to Berlin and thought we were making a fuss about nothing. [...]

Claus arrives in London at 7.15 next Saturday morning. I will meet him at the station and have given him full instructions on how to get the train. The train will bring him straight from Arbroath to London without having to change. I've sent him money for the journey and told him to begin to think out what he most wants to see in London – not that he will be able to see much in so short a time, but it will be an appetiser for his next visit.

I'm so glad the parcels are arriving all right. Now that I know that the flour does not go bad, I will send some more. This is easy, because I can get flour instead of bread with my bread coupons and I never need all of them.

We are having typical April weather here. An hour ago it was snowing. Now the sun shines brightly. I will write again soon.

Till then: All my love to all of you.

Your Tristan.

Tristan had meanwhile arranged for Marlene to move from her school in Zeven to a better one in Lübeck and to take over my room there. I think, but am not sure, that the Dregers paid her school fees and gave her free board and lodging – a rich West German family's gesture towards refugees.

A second letter my mother had saved (presumably Tristan sent her many more) was dated 23 April:

Dear Mutti and Omi,

I was glad to have your two letters. I was quite sure that Marlene would quickly adapt herself to her new life in Lübeck, and I am delighted to know that she has settled down so well. No one, I am sure, could be anything but happy in that nice room at Dregers.

Yes, Freyersen must certainly seem lonely for you now that the younger members of the family are away. But you do at least know each of them is living under better circumstances than the great majority in Germany today and that the outlook for their individual futures is a good deal brighter than it is for most young people in Germany today. If all of us use our heads wisely, I think we should be able to do a lot more for each of them – and, I hope, for you and Omi – in the years ahead. Things move very slowly, and we need to be patient, but there are quite a number of hopeful signs.

The fact that Anneli is still in Berlin is, of course, the biggest immediate problem. But, as I think you know, the problem is largely of Anneli's own creation. We have done all we can, and only her own obstinacy stands in the way! Perhaps I ought not to say that, but it is true!! She seems to imagine that everyone here at the

68

Observer is trying to make life more difficult for her. The truth is that people here have gone to great trouble simply in order to make sure that she can get out of Berlin safely. I will just give you two examples: The Observer was willing, if it would make it easier for her to get out of Berlin, to appoint her an official correspondent in Hamburg – that is, to give her an official reason for transport back to the British Zone. And The Observer obtained a promise from our Foreign Office here that if any German civilians had to be evacuated from Berlin by air, Anneli would be given a place in an aeroplane. This promise was given by Lord Pakenham personally. And there are several other things they did in order to fulfil their responsibilities for her safety. (All this information is confidential, by the way, and should not be passed on to other people. And Anneli does not know about any of it either. I knew it would do no good to tell her, but I will tell her later on when she is out of Berlin).

Well, Anneli is Anneli and she will have to learn that she is not always right about everything! I have the fullest sympathy for her feelings. No one here pretends that Frankfurt will be MORE interesting than Berlin. And I can quite understand that she prefers Prussians to South Germans. And that she prefers the weather in Berlin to the weather in the West – and so on. But the decision to move Stephens to Frankfurt was taken some time before all these disturbances in Berlin, and if Anneli wants to decide what the Observer should do with its own correspondents instead of letting it decide for itself, then she had better apply for the job as Foreign Editor!

I tell you all this so that you shall know the background to this great argument she and I have been having. I think she has calmed down now, and that she will come peacefully with Stephens when he leaves. (I think he is going to look for accommodation in the British Zone early next week). We have no doubt made some mistakes here, but they are mistakes born of goodwill towards her and not, as she likes to think, the opposite.

I hope you understand. Next time, if we feel she ought to leave some place I think we will just ask her to STAY at all costs and see what happens!!!

If you think we have acted wrongly, please tell me. We did what we thought was right in the circumstances.

I have sent off to you one or two more books today – including five of the Ro-Ro-Ro novels. I am afraid that these would soon fall to pieces if they are lent to other people, and we shall have to see if some kind of stronger cover can be made to protect them. Maybe I could get some cardboard and send it to you.

Would it be a good idea if I was to get a rubber stamp made here, which you could use to mark the books? If so, perhaps you could tell me what wording to use? Or, would it be better to get a small bookplate designed and printed which could be stuck into each book? Perhaps I am getting too ambitious too soon. But you must tell me of little things like this which I could do as soon as you think you have enough books to make a beginning with the library idea. Let me have all your ideas, won't you?

About food parcels: I am sorry that I have had so much work in these last few weeks that I have not managed to pack and post as many as I would have liked. But I have plenty of good things ready to send to you as soon as they can be packed up. I will post them and let you know.

And that is all my news for today. If you have NOT yet received the 350 RMs from Düsseldorf, please tell me. If they have arrived safely, don't bother. He says (provided, of course, that the things I write for him are satisfactory – which is by no means certain – that he will send you the next 350 about May 12.

Now goodnight and good wishes and much love to you both.

Always your Tristan.

P.S. Don't worry about the Flugzeuge which brummen – they are sent to encourage you and to discourage Mr Sokolovsky!!

I found these letters in my mother's hoard of letters, including mine, and diary notes when she died. Most of my account so far has been based on these. At roughly the same time I received a letter from Tristan's wife Mary, telling me that I was mistaken to believe him to be cruel, or too pedantic, let alone lacking in imagination or a true sense of humour. She was his wife, so she should know. Deep down he was a good, caring, imaginative man... The letter sang his praises as if she were trying to sell him to me. Tristan must have made her do it. She did NOT say that she was going to divorce him, nor did I want her to say that. I knew in any case that he had a flat of his own in Kilburn now while she continued to live in their old Hampstead flat. I did not like their separation, least of all the thought that I might have inadvertently caused it. In Lübeck Tristan had always assured me of his great love for his wife and had kept a framed photograph of the smiling, dark-haired woman in his room. I was sad that Mary wrote such a letter to me. But I was too occupied with politics to take much notice of it.

I was becoming more and more anti-American. I knew that the Americans did not want to start another war and would pull back from the brink. So why did they keep on with those stupid provocations?

Mrs Stephens went to another party in her stunning white gown and was lovely when she returned a little tipsy. Men adored her. This night Mr Colvin had been her dancing partner, and he stayed on for a chat and another drink. She was flattered by such adoration; it was all good fun. I was sure that Graham Smith, an actor from the opera Peter Grimes, also admired Mrs Stephens, but the most infatuated man of all was Rex Warner, author of 'The Professor', which Tristan had read to me once, and also of 'The Aerodrome', the novel from which the author himself read parts when we drank wine on the terrace of our new house in Fontanestrasse.

The Russian sector

While still living in Hohenzollerndamm, we again went to interview people in the Russian sector, asking the same idiotic questions again and again. There was an exhibition on 1848 in one of the buildings. The very word 'revolution' is anathema to Reid. Yet he blames the Russians for their lack of open minds to different ideas. We saw a teacher with a group of children at the Kaiser Wilhelm Monument and wondered what she was telling them. In Weissensee Park we saw many children cycling and tried in vain to interview them. There were soldiers singing while marching, with their beautifully deep Russian voices.

Reid was urging Pohlman to drive "as close as possible" to the Russian headquarters at Karlshorst. Then we had a shock, because we were stopped by a sentry, beckoning us to stand on one side inside the huge compound. Soon a Russian car drove towards us, beckoning us to follow. Reid was really scared, wondering if he should eat his notes. Pohlman suggested that the inside of his socks would not be searched and from his shoulders I could see how he was laughing. I nearly burst out laughing myself when I saw Reid's struggle with shoes, socks and notes. He had only just hidden the notes when the car in front of us stopped and one of the men jumped out to open the door next to Reid. Mr Reid looked so pale, I felt almost sorry for him. The Russians clicked their heels to attention and saluted: "What can we do for you?"

Reid recovered his composure, explained that we had not come to interview anyone, "but now we are here, could we see Marshal Sokolovsky"? They replied with a big laugh. Amidst more laughter and glasses of vodka we were invited to their office and then given a guided tour of most of the camp.

Later in the afternoon we went to see 'Young World in Old House' in the Brecht theatre on Schiffbauerdamm. Mr Stephens returned from Finland and went to the opera with Reid.

A few days before the Reid interviews Lori and I had decided to go to the House of Soviet Culture. We walked up a grand, carpeted staircase and entered the door marked 'surgery'. A fragile, but not unattractive officer rose from his seat behind a large desk and beckoned to us to sit on two chairs before he sat down again. He seemed a very polite, well-educated man, discussed the world's societies with us, frequently quoting Mark Twain. Knowing only the funny bits of that author, I could not contradict the Russian's statements. I noticed that he had beautiful slim hands and a gentle expression on his face. Was he Jewish? Or Asiatic? I determined to go again to work out the answers to these and many more questions. I asked for his name and he bowed to introduce himself as Mikrovitch[11]. We in turn told him our names and said we would come again on the next surgery day.

Lori did not find Mr Mikrovitch as interesting as I did, so she asked me to go on my own. When I came into the office he recognized me and offered me a cigarette. I had thought up some more, hopefully tricky questions, but he always found the right answers. If I were not convinced about their system's freedom and absolute determination to receive criticism, I should come to a Trade Union meeting in the House on the following evening and listen to the way the delegate comrades spoke out. Then I could write my own critical letter to the largest newspaper of the Soviet zone, the Tägliche Rundschau.

I went to the meeting. He obviously saw me, but somewhat timidly – or was it proudly? – ignored me. Then I wrote a critical letter to the paper comparing the stage-managed event with similar meetings in capitalist countries.

I was so absorbed in Thomas Mann's 'Doctor Faustus' which Mr Stephens had given me that I hardly noticed how the week had gone. I found Thomas Mann even more difficult to read than Virginia Woolf or Proust. So I was surprised when my reply from the communist newspaper came, but not surprised by the contents,

---

[11] Possibly a typo for Mirkovich

politely expressing pleasure at my writing, but regretting that they did not have space to print it. I took this reply to the House of Soviet Culture.

Mikrovitch looked at it and believed that the lack of printing space was genuine. Then I dared Mikrovitch to accept an invitation to the house of the Observer correspondent. "Why, don't you trust us?"

"Of course, I trust you. We Russians are not suspicious people. There always must be trust. But there is no time."

"Perhaps another day? A Sunday?" "Maybe..." was his answer.

I tried to discuss Tolstoy, because I had looked up provocative quotes. But I could not catch that man out, he answered all my quotes with counter quotes to 'put my statements into perspective', as he put it. How I wished that I were better educated and a quicker thinker. I could only think of replies I should have given when I am on my way home.

Hannelore told me that her parents wanted to send her to the West. Lori said that she would also like to do that if we all left, but because she was looking after all the Schneider family, she could not. Her mother Gretel would not survive a move away from the place that had been her home since Lori, Eberhard and Evi were born.

Da neigt sich die Stunde und rührt mich an
mit klarem metallenem Schlag:
mir zittern die Sinne. Ich fühle: ich kann –
und ich fasse den plastischen Tag.

The bell beats the hour; its unmuffled metal moves me,
My senses shiver, and now I know: the day is mine to mould.

Rilke (Das Stunden-Buch)

73

Moving house

Instead of moving to the West, we moved to a grand house with a huge garden in Fontanestrasse. The children were particularly delighted to have a garden at last. The house was built directly onto the street, so the drawing room windows towards the street were very small and high, while three French windows occupied most of the wall towards the garden, which sloped towards the lake below, where there were some trees and a boat house. Mrs Stephens was particularly pleased to find a good sailing boat there, so that she could sail across the lake to the Buschmanns' house on the other shore. But more often than not Mr Buschmann came in his boat to visit us.

With Nicky and Chimpy in the new garden

Next to the drawing room the house had a slightly smaller dining room from where one pair of French windows led to the terrace. Here we had an open fireplace in the wall at the outer extremity of the terrace, at right-angles to the house. Sometimes we lit it at night, even though nights were warm now. Rex Warner read poetry to us, or he and his wife Frances sang Greek love songs to each other, as they had seen couples do in restaurants in Greece. I loved their singing in the romantic setting of Fontanestrasse. They seemed such a happy couple, but later I gathered from Mrs Stephens that Frances Warner was very unhappy, Years later I learnt that Rex had fallen in love with a Rothschild lady, or with her money. He eventually married her.[12]

I did not understand how he could do such a thing to his wife or to his children. Anna, the eldest, had a mental disability, but George, who was only a few years older than Chimpy, seemed a normal, robust boy. On 23 April George celebrated his name day. I was not sure if this was a British celebration of their patron saint or if the Warners were Catholics.

Next day we adults celebrated Mrs Stewart's birthday with tea on the banks of the Havel.

Our rations ("Russians") arrived at the kitchen door, which opened fairly wide from a wall at right angles to the street. At the same side a ramp led down to a garage which we rarely used, as Pohlman had his own parking facilities.

The kitchen was a long room with windows looking out to the drive in the West. So it was particularly light in the evening. From here Roger could see the 'Russians' arrive and Nicky, now six months old, could sit in a high chair saying "Oh Gott, Gott Gott!" while our cook Frau Wenzel fed him. Later in England Nicky's sole German phrase, accompanied by sad shaking of his head, caused much amusement.

I continued with my weekly visits to the House of Soviet Culture. Mr Warner and Stephens had gone to Hanover. On their return, they told us that a Russian general had defected to the West from Bremen. When I confronted Mikrovitch with this news, he said that defection was the same as abduction, because America had not been devastated by war, so it was easy to bribe Russians with the prospect of life in America. I wondered if he himself could be tempted by such a prospect. He found that idea insulting and vigorously denied it. So why did he not dare to visit us in Fontanestrasse? I gave him our telephone number in case he changed his mind.

On my birthday I felt awfully old. To have reached the quarter century point seemed depressing, but I cheerfully accepted phone calls and visitors, picnics on the Stöbensee, dinner in style, even the prospect of Sebastian Haffner being sent to 'support' Stephens' reporting.

As I went to the next consulting hours at the House of Soviet Culture, I noticed that I was being watched by three men as I walked up those grand stairs. In the surgery room everything began as usual: the offer of a Russian cigarette after I had taken my seat, the beginning of our conversation… but then I heard the door open behind me. An officer entered. Mikrovitch jumped up and stood to attention. I noticed that his fine hands were shaking and dared not look higher. The two men conversed in their own language, which always sounded like music to me, music without meaning. Then Mikrovitch bowed to me to apologize because he was called to attend to other business, but hoped to see me again one day. I rose from my chair, feeling almost as shaky as he seemed. As I was trying to walk down the flight of stairs with as much dignity as I could muster, I saw a Red Army officer leaning over the rails, to watch me go, still leaning and looking when I crossed the carpeted hall. Be quick but proud, I told myself as I reached the outside door and turned to the right. I heard a window open on one of the upper floors and looked up to see that same officer again; the same thing happened when I had reached the corner and turned right, alongside this palace. I crossed the road, disappeared from the

---

[12] A decade later he remarried Frances.

observers' sight under the Friedrichstrasse underground bridge and felt totally relieved when the train crossed the border of the Russian sector.

Rumours began to circulate in the press club: Mikrovitch had disappeared and nobody knew where to, nor even what kind of story the Russian authorities would tell the press. On my return to the house our cook told me that there had been a phone-call for me. "He spoke in a Russian accent, but left neither a message, nor even a name. He might possibly ring again." I waited in vain for such a call.

Nützen muß man den Augenblick, der einmal nur sich bietet.

Make the most of the moment: it presents itself only once.

Schiller (Dom Karlos)

Towards Crisis in Berlin

The party-studded life went on – all the usual people with General Herbert as an additional host.

From 6 May onwards I swam regularly in the Berlin lakes and explored Grunewald by bike on my own. My cousin Rolf, whom we had nicknamed 'Mops', came to visit me for a few days and was as much fun as ever, though slightly more arrogant now. Apart from the Stephenses, I liked my own company best, but often felt lonely and worried about our future.

I had borrowed a spade from Frau Wenzel and began to do some gardening. M. de Turenne suggested turning part of the lawn into a more practical vegetable patch. He did most of the hard digging. Mrs Stephens planted many tomato plants, 70 celeriac, then ten larger tomatoes.

The Stephenses arranged for me to fly to Hamburg before going to my mother. I was excited about this, my first flight and the airport atmosphere.

In Freyersen I began to lengthen old dresses to give them the now fashionable 'new look' and to sew new ones out of old curtains. The latter did not look in the least like old curtains, and I was sure I could walk along the Kurfürstendamm in them, competing with the American ladies.

But travelling back to Berlin by public transport had become extremely difficult. So, by phone, it was arranged for me to have a lift from a friend of David Astor's in his private plane and so re-enter Berlin illegally. Avoiding the passenger lounge I sneaked on to the tarmac and into the small plane. The pilot gave me a piece of chocolate to chew in case things turned out bumpy, but, just as the plane had started to roll forward a little, it received a radio message from the control tower, saying that 'the girl seen to board the plane must come out at once'. To avoid the cost and effort of switching the engine off, the second man simply opened the large doors, helped me to jump and threw my big suitcase after me. So there I was, a lone figure on the wide tarmac, dragging my suitcase – with all my new dresses – across the airport. I felt miserably lost as I struggled to hitch-hike back to Freyersen. I had no West German after-curfew pass, and the only way I knew back to Freyersen was along the motorway, where it is always forbidden to hitch-hike. As it grew dark and the car headlights went on, I could not tell who was a potential patron of hitch-hikers or who was military police. Most of the time I crouched and dragged my case below the bank, only sometimes I found a car looking really private, so that I dared to climb up and wave my thumb. Eventually I was lucky and at 4 a.m. reached my mother's room, where I fell asleep almost at once.

In the morning I phoned Berlin and was told that the Russians now required special passes for cars at Helmstedt, on the road to Berlin. Nevertheless, it was arranged that Sebastian Haffner, who was in Hamburg just then and planning to drive to Berlin, would fetch me in Freyersen next day. We still could not quite believe that the Russians had closed the borders without warning. East Germany had just been declared an independent republic.

So off we went, suitcase and all, and down I went, suitcase and all, when we discovered that the stories of closed borders were true. All that Mr Haffner could say to me was that I would have to make my own way from the border, because he was 'not all that British' himself. He struck me as rather scared, though he did not admit that.

Miserable and penniless, I watched him drive through the controls with apparent ease. I was about to beg for a few marks to phone for advice, when an American jeep stopped and, hearing my story, told me to jump into the back and lie still, similar to Vera among the sacks of potatoes. These American soldiers firmly refused the Russian request for their jeep to be searched and moreover asked me to sit up and show myself as soon as we had passed the border posts, whereupon, foot on the accelerator, off we went at great speed. I did not see Haffner's car on the road, but by the time he phoned the Stephenses to apologize for having abandoned me, I was there to answer the phone. Triumphantly, of course, because I really hated him on that day. But next day, hypocrite that I am, I accepted his invitation to visit his old mother, who had stayed behind when he emigrated to England.

She was a charming old lady, living in a very middle-class flat full of little lace mats, dainty teacups and pretty biscuits. She talked in an educated, slightly Jewish accent.

A currency reform was imminent. So I went on a spending spree with my remaining Reichsmarks; a pair of spectacles for my mother cost 93 Marks, a dressmaker's bill to use up a few more curtains, was 400 Marks. I also bought a beautiful edition of Goethe's 'Westöstlicher Diwan' for Marlene and me, a volume of 'Eugen Onegin' and one of Pushkin's poems in translation for my mother plus kitsch books for her lending library, an edition of 'Romeo and Juliet' for Marlene and almost the entire works of Shakespeare in translation for my cousin Usch.

When the currency reform came, I felt sure that it would widen the gap between rich and poor in West Germany, where people had been allowed to keep their old bank accounts while they were closed in the East in 1945. Those with bank accounts could now get currency in D-Marks at the rate of 1:10. So the rich should gain considerable sums, while in the East, more fairly, people would remain evenly poor, as would the refugees in the West, who had also lost their savings and bank accounts, One could not expect the West to make arrangements that might conceivably be interpreted as 'levelling' = communist equality. Oh! what the hell. Better to do farm work in return for a sack of potatoes than become obsessed with money and such vulgar calculations, I decided; but I knew I was lucky, that I had no right to lay down the law for others. The idea of having enough money to get fat in comfort was simply ghastly to me. But at that time, in mid-June 1948, I did not even trust the new D-Mark-to-be; it seemed hardly worth having.

When I tinkled well-remembered Russian tunes on the piano, or watched Russian children play in Weissensee Park, I could have howled in pain. It helped a little to watch the setting sun behind the trees from our terrace, to imagine the lake glowing red in the reflected light, and the birds singing their own *kleine Nachtmusik*. But sometimes such beauty intensified rather than eased the pain. It also helped to watch Chimpy and Trixy play such imaginative games. We adults could learn such a lot from them.

Berlin blockade

On 22 June I remembered the day in 1941 when the Soviet Union was invaded by German planes and troops. Some girls in the Labour Service camp turned astrologers, saying that Mars was very red and close to Jupiter and that this boded blood and evil. We had all been scared, just as now, six years later, I was scared. It all seemed so silly and unnecessary. When I heard a broadcast of the town delegates' assembly, I cried myself silly. Poor Frau Schröder, so good and sensible, coping with such a job! In spite of my sympathies for many of the demands by the SED and the Russians, I did admire Frau Schröder's calm and almost friendly resistance. Perhaps women make better politicians than men? At least she did not allow dogma to cloud her reactions.

In all this confusion I sometimes forgot to water the tomatoes.

Our Grunewald home, and the tomatoes we could never harvest
To the right is the terrace where Rex Warner read to us

On 24 June Mr Stephens asked me to walk along the streets, listening to people's conversations and making notes. It was refreshing to re-discover the Berliners' brand of humour. On the black market 1 D-Mark was selling for 5 Ostmarks. But people had a calm, wait-and-see attitude. "All big promises, let's see who keeps them." Or "At least we will now work for money instead of scraps of paper."

In the Russian sector the new currency came into effect on the 24th, while in the West it was only officially recognized on the 25th. On the 24th the Russian sector newspaper cost 2 RM (= Reichsmark = old currency) while those in the Western sector cost only 20 Pfennige. I knew that the next day I would get 60 DM for the 75 RM I still had, and my DM-papers would have a B for Berlin stamped across them.

On 24 June the military administration of the Soviet Zone cut off the electricity supply to the Western sectors. The West still had coal for a while, but some electricity works cut their production, just in case. Traffic police waved their arms about instead of the traffic lights switching green, amber, red. The exercise would not do these men any harm.

A broadcast of an SDP rally was very moving. Fortunately Lori came and brought me down to earth with some silly political jokes. She was fun, but it was hard to imagine what would become of her. She hated her place of work and all those pompous, enthusiastic SED puppets working with her, but had to think of her family. Unable to plan for the distant future, we planned for the next few days – for instance trips on Lori's own boat on the Spree.

I wished that my mother could have come, that on the day when I had to accept a lift from the Americans, she would have tried her luck with me at Helmstedt.

West Berlin had supplies for about another 30 days. Then what? The communists certainly could not starve the Berliners into submission; in fact their tactics were having quite the opposite effect. But would Allied transport planes be used to transport people West in a mass evacuation operation, or did they really hope to supply West Berlin with food and fuel for an indefinite period? It was certainly interesting, and I told myself that the Stephenses' acceptance of me was the most wonderful thing that had happened to me. I was grateful for my Observer job, but more than anything for Chimpy and the beautiful place we lived in. Hypocrite that I am when I scorn riches and 'the rich', I did enjoy the beautiful voices of Rex Warner and Mr Stephens when they read to us, the charming giggles of Mrs Stephens, particularly when she was tipsy in a beautiful evening dress, Baby Nicky was growing into a real person by the hour. Our tomatoes were beginning to show patches of colour. Soon we would no longer depend on my ration cards for fresh vegetables, nor on Lori, constantly bringing us fresh ones from her allotment.

Some days were really hot and sultry. When Mr and Mrs Stephens went sailing, we swam in 'our' lake. Not very clean, but cool enough.

Sometimes Lori spent the night with us and we talked until the early hours about politics and about the benefits of close family relations versus freedom.

Beginning of the Berlin airlift

One day I had to translate a long, detailed two-year plan from 'Neues Deutschland', pages and pages of waffle. I approached Mr Martin's secretary for help, but smart-looking girls often lack a smartly-working brain, so I struggled on. Lori came to visit again, and as I had no time to go to the cinema, she spent the night with me in our house and we played chess in bed until sunrise.

On the first of July, after I had collected my food rations, I was told that I could fly in a transport plane to Wunstorf. A large crowd of journalists had gathered at the airport in order to report on General Robertson's opening of the Berlin airlift. It was a bumpy flight across clouds and air-pockets. I was allowed to sit next to the pilot, who gave me some plain chocolate to chew to prevent sickness.

Next morning I wrote my report on Wunstorf, then read articles in various papers, most of them saying that it would not work for long and that the Wunstorf population did not have enough food for themselves, anyhow; so there might be looting. We began planning our flight to England. We did not want to leave our tomatoes before they were ripe, yet it was quite exciting for me to go to a foreign country. I urged the Kowalewskis to visit us while we were still in Berlin. Jutta did come, introducing me to her fiancé, Heinz, and doing some shopping in Berlin which still offered more than other East German towns.

Mr Stephens (I still hesitated to call him Bob, as most people did) was busy studying the new currency legislation. Control of finance was expected to become entirely Russian.

Kressman was replacing Klingelhöfer. I liked both a lot and felt sorry for them all. Who would bother about them in the end? Was this a futile last stand? Already there were hardly any D-Marks in circulation in Berlin.

A DPD photographer called Maak, who had been on the flight to Wunstorf, kept visiting and phoning me, sending or personally presenting beautiful bouquets. He was quite a pleasant man but bored me after the first few minutes.

Between entertaining Jutta and Heinz and reading and translating gloomy papers I had to dash from one office to another for my visitor's visa to England, which I did not really want. But what were the alternatives? The Observer refused to employ me in Berlin, and in Berlin I saw no way of supporting myself. All the time I had bouquet-laden visits from Maak. Sometimes he only phoned, which was boring enough.

Electricity restrictions were becoming more frequent. Sometimes S-Bahn trains were not running at all. I was now more occupied with translations than with Chimpy, which was rather sad. So, perhaps, it was just as well that I was given a visa in York House.

Lori and Hannelore came for a farewell dinner, which we cooked ourselves, using fresh spinach. The Bulgarians, Lynn with Henry, the Warners and many others came. Pohlman and Frau Wenzel said they hoped we would return soon, which I was sure even they did not believe.

Zukunft hast du mir gegeben,
Doch du nahmst den Augenblick,
Nahmst der Stunde fröhlich Leben,
Nimm dein falsch Geschenk zurück!

You gave me a future,
But you took the moment,
Took the hour's joyous life,
Take back thy false gift!

Schiller (Kassandra)

Flight across another border

14 July 1948

Dearest Mutti, Marlene and Omi,
I imagine you'll already be sitting in Freyersen, loyally united, when this letter arrives, so I'll leap straight in... I've been in London since the night before last, and honestly don't feel like I'm abroad at all, apart from the excitement about everything driving on the left. That's probably because thanks to the Stephens, I was used to English to-and-fro anyway, and German guests speaking English.
Let's start at the very beginning.
We set out at 6 p.m. on Monday. Chimpy was just crazy with excitement, but fortunately in a nice sense. When we got onboard he must have shouted "I'm in a plane!" at least ten times. As it climbed, he simply couldn't get rid of his amazement, beaming at everything. We were sitting in the first row, in front of the wings, so could see just as well as those behind, watch the propeller and, even more interestingly, see the wheels retract after take-off and drop down again before London. Chimpy sat at the window, I next to him (facing backwards). Opposite me was Mrs Stephens, and opposite Chimpy – Mummy, you'll be jealous – an Indian, who was very, very nice and looked fantastic. Against all expectations we flew via Hamburg with a stopover for tea in the airfield's large and modern restaurant. I was just as crazy with joy as Chimpy, although I now know the landscape between Berlin and Hamburg almost by heart. To my shame, I must confess that having completed three flights, the thought of uncomfortable car, train, or ship journeys makes me feel a little tingly. I certainly wouldn't object to winning a big dollar denominated lottery.
The flight got really interesting after Hamburg, and the geographical knowledge of both Mrs Stephens and myself were quite disgraceful! While we were over Germany, we hadn't the faintest idea – you could have told us we were over the Black Forest, and we would have smiled coyly. Even the densest of people would have been able to recognize the border between Holland and Germany, however, because the straight lines in Holland are just unbelievable. Not even the smallest forest paths make curves, every tree in the forest seems to be planted with a compass & ruler at a set distance from each other. I never expected it all to be so precise. As we came over the Zuider See, Mrs Stephens & I admired loudly and audibly our view of the 'North Sea', and I even felt quite strange flying towards the coast of 'England', until we both raised our heads (the other passengers looked politely sideways) and blushed, seeing the slip being circulated to announce that Amsterdam was 15 miles below us to the left. We therefore decided to admire the real North Sea in silence! By the way, it was sunset when we flew over the sea, and the picture was indescribable. A mixture of light, water, air and reddish clouds – you couldn't see where one merged into the other and so you floated in the middle of space in the happy feeling that God hadn't even created the planets yet – I mean, there was sunlight but no sun, water but no sea. Oh, you just have to experience it all for yourself!

BEA FLIGHT BULLETIN

From Captain _P R COLE_ _to all passengers_

RMA _PIONAIR 'BENTFIELD HUCKS'_

TIME

London time is _1651_ Local time in _PARIS_

POSITION _ABBEVILLE_

HEIGHT		**SPEED**			
		AIR SPEED		CORRECTED FOR WIND (SPEED OVER GROUND)	
_6500_	Feet	_165_	m.p.h.	_160_	m.p.h.
_2000_	Metres	_265_	k.p.h.	_257_	k.p.h.

INFORMATION

We are now _90_ miles from _PARIS_ At _1715_

hours we pass _CROSS de ENGLISH COAST_ miles to our right/left. We call next at

LONDON arriving there at approximately _1750_ LOCAL GREENWICH time.

NOTES

The traffic officer who will meet you on landing will be glad to assist you in any way he can.

The name of your Steward/Stewardess is _MISS BOSSIT_

PLEASE PASS ON QUICKLY

BRITISH EUROPEAN AIRWAYS

Some slips can cause slip-ups

Oh yes, we'd eaten dinner shortly before. Chimpy's and my eyes almost fell out of their sockets when our little tables were opened out & the plates brought to us. 'mock rabbit' meatloaf, corned beef, cucumber salad, green salad, pickles – pudding (custard in layers of different colours, decorated with buttercream) – rolls, butter, cheese – coffee. And then we smoked away the feeling of fullness.

Chimpy and Nicky were both wide awake but agreeable. Although Nicky hadn't slept since 12am, he didn't cry once, just crowing and yelping loudly. Chimpy's mouth was never still either, and in the late evening we couldn't stop him from making expeditions throughout the plane (except the pilot's cabin & kitchen). He enjoyed it immensely, as the thick carpets meant that falling over didn't seem as horrible as at home.

Then we were really over England, which lay below us in a dusky green with streaks of water through it. Gradually the lights came on and we flew in circles over London, which seemed to me like a fantastic sea of light, despite the electricity shortages here.

At the airport, I was treated completely as a foreigner, i.e. better than the English passengers. I was already beginning to doubt whether I might have dollars in my pocket instead of Deutschmarks. At the exit stood — John! Wasn't that nice? You

can't get to the airport[13] without a car. But for that reason, we didn't accept John's offer of a lift, but hurried via the Air Service bus to where Tristan & Mrs Stephens's sister were waiting for us. We then continued by taxi to Mrs Jerome & Stephens.

The Jeromes have a very nice & comfortable flat, with great furniture. On Monday night we just drank sherry & coffee then went to bed.

Everything here literally radiates culture, very good crockery, tablecloths, flowers, etc. Mr Jerome is a lawyer & studied for two semesters at Heidelberg (just for fun: German law in itself has no professional value for him in England). I find them both quite touching.

On Tuesday Tristan came to pick me up after breakfast. We went to the Stephenses for a bit, then to the bank, then spent most of our time doing History & Culture until I was dead tired and street names, personalities and buildings were spinning wildly around my head. Westminster Abbey in particular is very tiring because it's so big and so many names press in upon you. What I liked best amongst the old militarists were the two soldiers from the Life Guards in their old uniforms, standing motionless, high on their steeds(!) at their post in front of Buckingham Palace. Tomorrow at 11 a.m. there's always supposed to be some kind of big parade for the new guards. I have to see that for myself. By the way, the King was present (his flag was up), but I didn't see him.

At Downing Street I was really quite shocked, because the houses of the Prime Minister & the Chancellor of the Exchequer look anything but splendid. St James's Park nearby is very pretty though, and I'm half determined to get up at 5 a.m., to be there at 6 a.m. when Cripps[14] – the so-called "Spartan" & apparently most respected man in Parliament – and Attlee go for their traditional morning walks. But that's for later.

There is so much on display in the shops that you can hardly see it all. But the prices!!! Hair-raising! The fruit on the stalls in the streets is probably the prettiest thing here, next to the red buses. But a really nice peach, for example, is 8d, which is about 1.40 Dmarks according to the official exchange rate (for travellers). Cigarette prices are incredibly high. (But I did buy some this morning, because it's so much fun to buy something like that freely.)

On Tuesday afternoon, Tristan & I had tea at his flat, which, incidentally, made me weep with laughter. The funnel gramophone! The fish (which just happens now to be dressed up in an elaborate Stalinesque shopping net)! The picture gallery! But one thing has to be said about Tristan: the world has lost a good painter. The flat looks very tidy & friendly, although it's still missing many things to make it truly furnished. The Guttmanns[15] are in Switzerland at the moment, but will be back on Sunday. Little Monika is very cute. Incidentally, I am now of the opinion that Marlene could live there very well, because the rooms of Tristan's flat are, so to speak, completely mixed with Guttman's flat. Tristan's kitchen, for example, is linked to Guttman's kitchen & none to his two rooms. Those two rooms also have

---

[13] Northolt Airport

[14] Sir Stafford Cripps, Chancellor of the Exchequer – despite his 'Spartan' keep fit regime, he resigned due to ill health two years later.

[15] Tristan's neighbours: Willi Guttmann was a Jewish German lawyer working for the Observer

no connection with each other, but are separated by the corridor through which all the inhabitants of the house enter. So it would be as if Marlene had rented an extra room at Guttmann's, where she would have lunch anyway. However, what Tristan's father would prefer is for Claus, Marlene & I to live with him in Aberystwyth, Claus & I to go to college & Marlene to school, and for me to look after the house, since the housekeeper carries out well whatever she is told directly, but does nothing of her own accord, so after the death of Dr Jones's sister he'll need a woman in the house in Aber. If only I didn't long so much for Germany and especially Berlin, that would be very nice. But just today I read so much again about the Berliners during Eden's stay there, and feel terribly shut off from everything German. Hopefully we'll go back to Berlin in September. I'm only really beginning to love the sad, defiant ruins of Berlin now I'm here, where so few houses are "blitzed". The sense of togetherness in Berlin, its longing for freedom cannot be outweighed by any glitzy London lights and shop windows.

Plan of 49 The Avenue, Kilburn

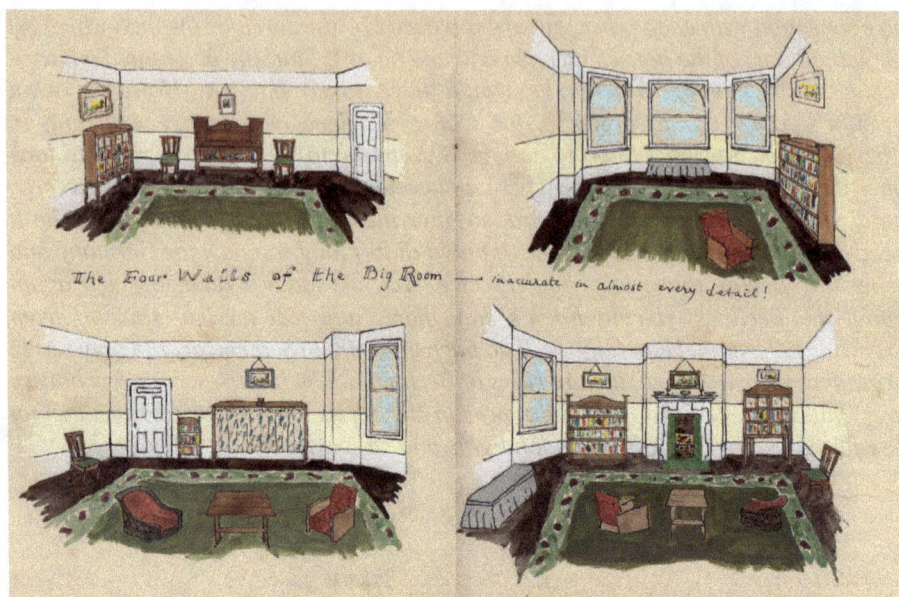

The Four Walls of the Big Room — inaccurate in almost every detail!

Tristan's 'Big Room'

The welcome cake I ate at Tristan's contained three of the eggs Claus always sends the Guttmanns.

In the evening I telephoned Claus, who sounded terribly happy. He now rides young horses in, every evening. He won't be here until 1 August. He could come on the night of the 1st, but would prefer to travel through the countryside in daylight. The following Monday he has to leave again. I'm really looking forward to it.

For dinner on Tuesday we were invited here to Jeromes. Wonderful! A table like we had at home in the ladies' room, set with pretty round doilies on top for the plates, small doilies in the same pattern for the wine glasses & medium doilies in the same pattern to the left, for the breakfast plates. Wonderful porcelain! The food was a kind of 'mock rabbit' in round slices with one piece of dried ham & two round slices of mushroom as garnish, pea purée & potatoes (oh yes, the slices of meat garnished with ham and mushrooms were on macaroni). Then delicious preserved cherries with custard in crystal bowls, followed by bread, butter, camembert (green & stinky, but delicious). Before dinner we had sherry, at dinner red wine as a "Welcome to England" toast for me. After dinner coffee & confectionery in the drawing room.

Today I'm going to Stephens for lunch and Tristan's for dinner. Ha ha, in the morning I want to dare to go shopping for some little things. I just hope people won't always give me the exact opposite of what I want. I'm sure I'll take even the biggest misunderstandings in my stride, for a fee, rather than get into long discussions in funny dialects.

Another funny thing. On the one hand, the English have sooo much laxer so-called morals than we do in Germany – even posh people like those here & T's father, for example, think it's strange that I don't live there with Tristan. On the

88

other hand, they are sooo against public nightlife that it's hard to get a bus or underground after half past eleven, impossible after twelve, and even taxis only with difficulty. No pub is open longer than 12, and very few are supposed to be open on Sundays (except for proper food restaurants) – even fewer sell alcohol.

So, happy & adventurous & full of longing for you, and for Berlin, Berlin, Berlin, I send many greetings to all.

Your Anneli

England

Tristan had come to meet us. He helped us move all our belongings to the basement flat in Camden Town where Bob's family lived. I spent my first night in London in the house of Bob's friendly mother, who was ever so pleased to see her son's family safely home, as were all his sisters, nephews and nieces. At least my impression was that there were many, though later on I could only remember Bobby and Jane. They all played happily in the small back garden which was surrounded by some flower beds with a washing line at one side and a large sand-pit at the back. The children played there in summer sunshine while we adults took cups of tea on chairs along the wall of the house. Bob's mother was now retired from her factory work, but very energetic in the house, a perfect granny, or "Nan", as the children called her.

I was happy to accept a sofa for the night. Tristan told us that on the following day he would take me to some of the famous sights of London and introduce me to his father's former secretary, who had married a lawyer and lived in Cleveland Square, not far from Paddington Station. I was invited to be their guest, but also offered the choice of the Rintouls' flat in the same house, because the couple were away on holiday. I was sad not to stay with the Stephenses, but understood that in that crowded house I would have been one person too many.

Bob took me to the Observer office in Tudor Street and introduced me to the editor, other Observer journalists, then left me in the news service office, where Ken Obank was editor and Tristan his assistant. The Observer printing presses were larger than those I had seen in the basement of the News Guardian, and the large number of offices was impressive. It was hard to imagine that in a few years' time they would prove too small.

Tristan took the afternoon off and invited me to lunch in one of the Fleet Street pubs, I think it was called 'The Feathers'.

Walking along Fleet Street I saw St Paul's Cathedral and at the other end the law courts. We walked all the way to Trafalgar Square, past so many famous buildings that I could not take them all in, but I was impressed with Nelson's Column and enjoyed having tea and a bun in Lyons' Corner House. I had seen enough for one day and was glad to sit on the top deck of a red bus which took us to Paddington.

Compared with Mrs Stephens' cosy, crowded, noisy house the Jeromes' flat was elegant and quiet. I liked Dick, the lawyer-husband, but mostly I liked Sybil, Tristan's father's former secretary who later told me much about Tristan's childhood in the shadow of his bright and lively brother Elphin, who had been run over while doing his Christmas shopping. Everybody admired Elphin's intelligence, and the sophisticated essays he wrote at school were published in a small book about him. Tristan, too, had admired and loved his little brother, but became morose in his presence and was not really liked by anyone. His mother did not long survive the shock of Elphin's death. Elphin had been very much her favourite and in need of special mothering, because he suffered badly from asthma and eczema. She did not seem to understand how much Tristan loved her. Sybil thought that everybody was cruel to Tristan. His behaviour began to make sense.

I spent one night in the Jeromes' guest-room, being treated to a cup of tea in bed in the morning, followed by a shower and a very English breakfast. What happened after that is a blur in my memory. I no longer know if it was on my first visit to London, or when Claus came later, or with Mutti, that we queued for an eternity to see the crown jewels in the Tower, or when I went to Speakers' Corner at Marble Arch, walked in Hyde Park, in St James' Park, on Hampstead Heath, saw Parliament and Westminster Abbey and listened to Tristan quoting Wordsworth on Westminster Bridge, not to speak of all those varied art galleries and museums. It was almost as exciting as Berlin, except for the absence of the children, who went to Taqui's old home in Aleppo soon after we had left Berlin. On the photos they sent I noticed that Nicky was growing up fast, but Chimpy did not seem to change.

I met Tristan's sister Eirene in a pub and later gathered from Tristan's father that she had been "favourably impressed" by me. She did not show it, but behaved like a very polite, formidable English lady. She was working as a lobby correspondent for some paper, but was hoping to stand for Parliament in the coming elections. If she won a seat, she would concentrate on her work, but if she did not, she and her husband John White planned to raise a family. When Eirene did win a seat for the Labour Party in the 1949 elections, I thought it a piece of divine providence with regard to potential children.

I also briefly met Tristan's father TJ in his Aberystwyth home Bryn Hir, on top of the hill, not far from the National Library of Wales. He was reserved in a friendly way. He told me that he did not approve of divorce – nor did I, of course – but he would give us a chance. (What was he talking about? I was still not considering marriage to Tristan and felt frustrated by all those assumptions around me.)

In Aberystwyth I was also introduced to the Principal of the university, Ifor Evans, whose wife Ruth was German-born and not that much older than me. She, together with her husband, TJ and Tristan discussed the best means of having Marlene come to Britain. They decided against a school and in favour of university, even though Marlene had not yet done her school-leavers' exam (*Abitur*) in Germany. They would give her a special university entrance exam. They also decided that she could live in TJ's house and that I should come to replace his present housekeeper, whom he did not like, "because she does not wash the inside of a teapot". I made a mental note of that and, of course, agreed to try my skill as a housekeeper. Aberystwyth looked a very beautiful seaside resort.

When I returned to my mother and sister in Freyersen to convey this news, I could hardly sort out my bubbling words. They thought I was joking when I mentioned university, but eventually I convinced them Marlene had to hurry to Aberystwyth for the entrance examination.

After Marlene had left – for her, too, this was the first flight of her life – I had to gather material to write an article about refugee life in West Germany for Servob, the Observer news service. As far as I know only one Australian paper bought it, but I was proud to have something published under my name by a good newspaper. I almost wished that someone whose obituary I had written would die. But no-one did.

After the excitements of Berlin and London, Freyersen seemed relaxing but boring. Christmas, however, was as beautiful as ever, and I felt sorry for Marlene experiencing British plum pudding and crackers, which we only had on New Year's Eve. I left for Aberystwyth, briefly interrupting my journey in London. The Stephenses were still in Syria.

West Germany welcomes the New Year – and drinks to a new war

(Article released on the Observer Foreign News Service wire and printed – in slightly edited form – in The Scotsman and the Belfast Telegraph, 6 January 1949, and the Sydney Morning Herald, 11 January 1949)

Celebrations   No. 2041   900 words   5.1.49
For ref: Filed Jan 3. – For Immediate Release
CONFIDENTIAL: the author of this article was until recently the secretary of our Staff Correspondent, Robert Stephens, in Berlin

West Germany welcomes the New Year – and drinks to a new war
Insoluble Clash Between the Dreams of the Old and the Hopes of the Young
By ANNELIESE WIEMER
A 25-year-old German girl from East Prussia, now a refugee in the British Zone of Germany

HAMBURG (By Airmail)

For the first time since 1945 the shops of WESTERN GERMANY offered crackers for the New Year celebrations. Lucky charms, confetti and a luxurious choice of drinks were all displayed in the windows. And despite the fantastic prices there was no lack of buyers.

For more than three years imports and German production had been restricted to the most urgent necessities of daily life. Currency reform has put an end to all that. Things whose very existence had been half forgotten are back on the market, though for the average German money is still very scarce.

But New Year celebrations are an occasion for recklessness, the one time of the year when everyone dismisses the usual calculations about which of the much-needed commodities are the most vital of all. With shopping bags, parcels and bottles, wrapped up in what the shops had left of Christmas packing paper, people thronged the main streets – streets tidier than at any time since war ended now that the new currency has made rubble clearance a remunerative occupation. The surface of Western Germany as the Old Year departed and the New arrived was colourful and gay.

Business men entertained lavishly in their homes. To accompany a good dinner they could offer unlimited champagne and Moselle, whisky and Benedictino, cognac and gin. The past months have swelled their bank accounts with the new money – money with the dollar behind it. Maybe this will not go on for ever. People have little money to save and are hesitant about putting their savings into the banks, with the result that the banks cannot give industry the credit it needs. Maybe there will be a slump. But who knows what the future may hold in store? Probably only the stars and the RUSSIANS – and to a certain extent the AMERICANS. Certainly we, the GERMANS, do not, so let us enjoy life while we may.

For three years now the occupation forces have been the only authorities, in the big and little affairs of daily life. They – the soldiers and the Control Commission men – were the people with chocolate and cigarettes, with coffee and cars. Now they have been left far behind by the German business men. And as the occupation forces now appear, by comparison, rather poor – particularly the BRITISH – they are no longer hated as they were. The dictionary of public complaints has substituted "the rich" for "the foreigners".

"We'll drink to a heavy tax on those who still don't know what it means to live in poverty": that was the New Year toast of many of the EAST PRUSSIAN farmers who abandoned their homes as the Russians approached in the last months of the war, and now live as refugees in the West.

The exiled farmer drinks his schnapps out of an egg-cup borrowed for the evening, and glances round his little room. One bed is used as a sofa during the day. The other is piled high with the bedding of the children who sleep on the floor. On a wooden packing case stands the Christmas tree, stolen from the woods. The farmer and his fellow-refugees raise their egg-cups and a happy, faraway look comes into their eyes. "to 1949 – and our first party back in East Prussia". There will be a third war, they believe, and the West will win – with the help of all the German refugees who will be fighting to regain the lost German lands in the East, fighting, as they persuade themselves, a crusade to carry culture to the uncivilised peoples who have taken their farms and homesteads. Such ideas are the main themes of the public gatherings of refugees, idea that keep hopes alive and do little to encourage initiative and hard work in the West.

The West Germans are glad, too. If war comes, the refugees who have been billeted on them will leave; there will be less competition to fear. All in the house, Westerners and Easterners alike, are happy at this time, drinking and dreaming of war.

A son of the refugee family sits reading in a corner of the room. He is studying at a nearby university town, paying his fees by clearing rubble from the bombed sites. He has come home to the small warm room (there are no longer any fuel restrictions in Western Germany) to welcome the New Year with his parents. He had looked forward to the reunion, but the conflict which divides many of refugee family, the clash between the dreams of the old and the hopes of the young, is insoluble. While his parents drink to a new war, he withdraws to the corner with his chemistry textbooks.

No new ideology has captured the mind of young Germany since the creed of HITLERISM was shattered. It is too early yet for German youth to face life with enthusiasm or confidence. But they are happy to have the chance to learn again, and the student son who hears his parents with mixed horror and pity is content to watch the New Year dawn with a chemistry book on his knee.

In the neighbouring room the owners of the house, Westerners, celebrate with cheap brandy and plenty of cakes. They play cards. Someone offers to tell fortunes. "The SOCIALISTS won't succeed with their plans for Lastenausgleich (equalisation of sacrifice – i.e. compensation for refugees, war widows, etc.), so you needn't worry about new taxes", he announces.

Hopes and fears are keen as the New Year opens. There is a feeling that 1949 will be a year of decision, of great events. What will it bring? Progress, or an end to life as we have come to know it? Some solution of the ever-present economic problems and social problems (though only the poor and a handful of idealists care about the latter), or greater hardship even than that experienced in those last three years? What may happen in "big politics" is not worth bothering about. A Constitution for Western Germany? What unnecessary fuss, what ridiculous farce when everyone knows that it is the dictatorship of the AMERICANS that will last and will count. And why shouldn't it last, as long as they dictate plenty of food? If only they would stop talking about how much they are giving us for nothing.

If they do not want to give us a receipt for all the German patents they have taken, that's all right. After all, they won. But why can't they stop all this humiliating talk about their generosity? Of course, such talk annoys people less now that it did in the first years. Now business absorbs all energies. To make money, some way, any way – that is all that matters. Germans of the West want more money to buy all the things in those shop windows. And, perhaps, rather more energetic action by the Americans so that the Russians really feel the power of the West. Because, when they stop dreaming and come to weigh it up, the Germans realise that peace has its advantages…

(Photo from Australian article)
"There are no longer any fuel restrictions in Western Germany, but in Berlin the Soviet blockade sends the women out with their handcarts, stripping bark to light backyard cooking fires."

Aberystwyth

I enjoyed Marlene's student friends, the company of TJ and his friends, as well as the unfamiliar job of a housekeeper. I was careful always to wash the teapot and did just enough cleaning without using the vacuum cleaner too much. When TJ thought it was his bedtime, he stretched out his legs, waiting for me to put on his slippers. He mostly drank tea, but had one glass of Claret every day, because his doctor had told him "not to drink alcohol except for a glass of claret". He had a beautiful voice with a pleasant Welsh accent which he seemed to use only when he was in Wales. In London he spoke in an upper-class English accent which suited a former civil servant and Downing Street secretary. He had served under four Prime Ministers, of whom, needless to say, he had liked Lloyd George best. The two men had often spoken Welsh together when they did not want others to understand what they were saying, he told me.

TJ spent much of the day working in his own library, sometimes going to the National Library when he did not have certain books at home. When he was in a jovial mood he read to us from the Mabinogion in Welsh, which I did not understand but enjoyed like music.

Every Sunday, and sometimes on Thursday as well, TJ went to the Welsh chapel half-way down the hill and urged Marlene and me to go to the English-spoken Presbyterian chapel in Bath Street. I really enjoyed those services, particularly the singing and the Rev. Griffith's intellectual sermons. I most vividly remember his sermon about the lilies of the valley not toiling yet pleasing God. He told us not to be self-righteous chapel-goers, but to forget about religion, even ethics, and walk along the beach, or in gardens, or forests, thanking God for sunshine, wind, waves. He and other Welsh people we met in Bath Street were very nice to us. One of the chapel's elders, Mr Edwards, often invited us to his own house for a cup of tea and biscuits with his wife, his son David and his daughter Lilian. Marlene became so interested that she chose theology as one of her university courses.

The professor of the theology faculty was one of TJ's many lady-friends. Another was Lili Newton, head of the biology department. Sometimes I had to make cakes, buns or scones for Sunday visitors to Bryn Hir. I liked some of TJ's friends, such as a neighbour called Caradoc Morris, a jolly, fat and intelligent man. Another occasional visitor was Dr Kurt Hahn, head of Gordonstoun School for boys, where Prince Charles later apparently did well in academic subjects and music; not so well in sports, which the school was famous for.

I also liked Joyce Grenfell, a cousin of David Astor's on his mother's side, who must have met TJ at Cliveden and was very fond of him. She was great fun, and after we had gone for a walk at Cwm Woods, she gave Marlene her green skirt, saying that actresses only wear such things once.

Marlene became president of the Overseas Students' Union and introduced me to many of her African friends, notably one handsome Egyptian who later made it to the top rungs in politics. He married Beryl, an American student.

I soon learnt the student tradition of 'kicking the bar', i.e. walking rapidly along the prom to the last bar across, giving it a kick and then turning. Occasionally we did not turn, but climbed over to bathe where the waves crashed vigorously on the shingles. On one such occasion, at night, a Danish girl student lost her diamond ring. We went to look for it in daylight and there it was, glinting in the sun among the pebbles.

Sometimes Marlene worked with her books while I typed stories on an old, heavy typewriter on the flat roof overlooking garden and library and, if we stretched, a small corner of the sea. When Mamushka received a visa to visit us, we took a small table into the high grass to have our coffee or tea on low cane armchairs – one of which I still have.

But, as it was spring when our mother came, we loved going for walks, climbing through wire fences to see a wonderful display of daffodils, part of a ruined estate garden alongside a grand but uninhabited house.

Good Friday was not a public holiday in this largely non-conformist country, where people thought of it as a Roman Catholic idea, similar to saints' days.

One day, when the tide was out, we nearly reached Clarach before we felt we should go back. But we were too late and found ourselves marooned by the tide in one small bay with very high cliffs behind us and rocks on either side. Marlene wanted to climb to the top and find someone to rescue Mamushka and a little dog which had come from no-where to join us. Fortunately a fisherman in his boat saw our dilemma and shouted that he could take the old lady and the dog, if they managed to scramble along the rocks to a place where the boat could safely pick them up. Our mother overcame her fear, but then was scared on Marlene's and my behalf. Marlene boldly crawled ahead of me, shouting when she feared she might dislodge a stone and occasionally allowing us some rest, leaning against the cliff wall. She even dared to look back and wave to my mother, who was travelling safely in the boat. Terrified, I tried to stop my knees from knocking against each other. But we did make it to the top, where we sat trembling in some grass before we walked towards the prom, where Mamushka was waiting for us. The relieved owners of the little dog had bought some fish from the man in the boat.

Meanwhile TJ was looking for a proper housekeeper to take my place when the Stephenses came back to Britain. He found a very good lady called Mrs Porter, who came to live with us even before I wanted to leave. We became good friends, and for a few mornings I too was given a cup of tea in bed in the morning.

Shark?

Marlene and I swam every day. Marlene had the awful habit of scaring me with seaweed, and one day, when she called out for help because "something was touching her legs", I only laughed: "Do you think it's a crocodile or a shark?" Something that looked like a big wooden post floated up to the surface before sinking into the water again, and the pained expression on Marlene's face convinced me that something was wrong. I allowed her to hold on to my shoulder while I swam back to land. Then I saw that her entire leg was red with blood and people came running along to support her. One lady who had her car near the beach took Marlene to hospital. I collected our clothes and walked back to TJ's house to wait. Fortunately TJ had gone to London and Mrs Porter was staying with friends in the Midlands. When Marlene was brought home with five parallel short lines of stitches along her leg, we decided not to tell TJ, so that he would not worry.

But TJ phoned soon after Marlene came out of hospital: he had read the story in the evening papers and was really frightened on Marlene's behalf. Of course, the papers were all guessing as to which creature might have bitten her. Sharks were known to have teeth which could not let go of a prey once it was in their mouths. So, maybe it had been a young whale? As I walked along the prom that evening I saw that the news had spread fast. People pointed to the horizon, where they claimed to see a whale spouting! A French newspaper guessed that it had been a giant conger eel, which sounded convincing. The German papers opted for a young shark despite the unlikely toothmarks. I wallowed in my sister's sudden fame, but phoned Freyersen to reassure my mother and Omi, who had already read the story. Marlene limped around with one bandaged leg, enjoying her fame. Two days later a young basking shark was washed ashore dead in Clarach, and the *Daily Mirror* chose the headline: 'Marlene poisons shark.'

FISH ATTACKS BATHER

GIRL'S ALARMING EXPERIENCE.

Tried to Pull Her Under.

GRIM STRUGGLE LONG WAY FROM BEACH.

A girl swimmer had an alarming experience at Aberystwyth, on Friday, when she was attacked by a large fish. In the struggle to ward it off she received several bites, and on reaching the beach was rushed to the hospital for treatment.

The girl, who was swimming a considerable way out from the shore, off Victoria-terrace, was Miss Marlene Wiemer, Brynhir, Penglais-road, Aberystwyth, who, with her sister, Anneliese, are often seen swimming at this spot.

Had Strong Hold.

On Friday afternoon, Marlene, who is a strong swimmer, was a long distance from the shore when she felt something grab her right leg below the knee and attempt to pull her under. It had such a strong hold that in the fight to brush it off, several gashes were made in her leg.

Showing great presence of mind she warned her sister to swim for the shore while she got rid of her attacker. Greatly weakened from the struggle and shock she arrived on the beach with blood streaming from her leg.

A member of their party, Mrs. S. Burke, fortunately had a car, and Miss Wiemer was taken to the Aberystwyth Hospital, where the bites were treated, one of them requiring stitches.

First Instance.

This is the first instance of a bather being attacked by a fish in this manner, but it should be made clear that the incident happened a long way out at a distance not normally reached by bathers and that no such fish have been reported in the area nearer the beach where the majority of bathing is done.

Miss Wiemer could not get a clear enough view of the fish to describe it in any detail. "I was so surprised by the attack and concerned with fighting it off by kicking and splashing that I had no time for anything else," she said.

Miss Wiemer has been in this country since January and is now awaiting the result of an examination following a course as a part time student at the U.C.W. Marlene and Anneliese are refugees from East Germany.

Shark attack newspaper clipping

The local papers, trying to limit the damage to their tourist industry, wrote that Marlene and I had frequently been warned by fishermen because we were always swimming more than a mile out to sea. Maybe they were right; one can't measure distances when enjoying a swim. For the next few days a curate friend of ours insisted on swimming parallel to us on the side of the open Atlantic, carrying a large carving knife between his teeth, which became uncomfortable after a while. Back on the beach that man shivered so much that I thought he was catching a cold, but he insisted he was fine.

The curate's wife, Margaret, also came to the beach sometimes, bringing her little son, who was pleasant, though not as bright as Chimpy. One day, when the curate was going to St David's Cathedral for his ordination, he suggested that I should come with Margaret, who could leave the son with her parents on a large country estate near St David's. The curate had to spend some time before the ordination in retreat. Margaret and I first travelled to her parents' house, which was grand, but slightly gloomy. Her father took us around the fascinating countryside, showing us the wild coastline and the grand cathedral. The ordination ritual was moving and much more beautiful than the simple services in Bath Street Chapel. Afterwards we celebrated with a champagne dinner, toasting the curate, who was now a proper priest.

Soon after our return to Aberystwyth I left for London, where I stayed in the Jeromes' flat for two nights before the Stephenses arrived. My mother had also spent two nights there before going back to Germany. Ration cards made it difficult to do much shopping, but Sybil somehow managed to give Mamushka that treat.

The Lake District

The Stephenses did not unpack all their luggage, because we were off to the Lake District two days after they returned from Syria. It was a long train journey. To while away Chimpy's and Nicky's boredom, Bob began to tell them stories: "Two men were travelling in a train like ours. They sat opposite each other. Then one asked the other 'Do you believe in ghosts?' 'No' replied the other, and vanished..." "So he was a ghost!" exclaimed Chimpy, and Nicky began to look around the carriage.

A taxi waited for us at Coniston station and drove us to the other side of the lake, along a climbing lane, up to Lanehead, a large house which reminded me of the novel *Jane Eyre*. We negotiated a maze of corridors upstairs. My room looked out on the lake and the mountains beyond, where the Old Man was hiding his head in the clouds. I had plenty of opportunity to see the summit later, as this summer of 1949 was a very dry, sunny one. The humorous postcards of people boating with umbrellas over their heads made no sense to me.

The drawing room downstairs was large and quite dark in spite of the French windows. From there we could see only the mountains, as the lake lay behind the large trees at the bottom of the lawn. This lawn swept downhill to a little gate hiding in bushes and from there to a path down to the boat house.

When we walked down the steep path to the two boat houses Taqui told me that she and her sisters and brother Roger had inspired Arthur Ransome, 'Uncle Arthur', to write his famous children's book 'Swallows and Amazons'. As there were four girls (Taqui, Bridget, Titty, Susan) and only one boy in the Altounyan family, Ransome had turned Taqui into a boy, so that his book would have the same appeal to boys as to girls. And there, over to our left, she pointed to a vaguely discernible Peel Island, which we would visit soon.

Looking across Coniston
Peel Island on the left. Arthur Ransome lived at the other end of the lake.

I was warned that the people who had rented the Lanehead Annex belonged to a peculiar religious sect who were calculating the end of the world by what they considered serious scientific means. One of the men reminded me so much of Herr Emde in Zeven, that I thought he must also be a Freemason. They were pleasant people and very nice to the children.

Next morning we heard rather than saw Donald Campbell practising for the water speed boat trials, so the lake turned rough and dangerous for sailors. We had our packed picnic at the edge of the lake, in a meadow near the boat houses. The children wanted to explore and look into the water "for minnows", but every time they walked along the landing stage, Bob called out repeatedly "Be careful!" Taqui thought he was undermining their confidence, but I too imagined that at any moment there would be the big splash of a child falling into the lake. Fortunately the boys became bored and joined us for a 'swim', really just splashing about while we swam in the hot sunshine. Sometimes the wash from the speedboat made little waves, which reminded me of Cranz on a calm day. We dried off in the grass, Taqui managing a siesta in the sun. Our picnic reminded Chimpy of a Beatrix Potter story and he wanted to catch "a big fat minnow" like that of Jeremy Fisher in his butterfly net.

When we climbed back to Lanehead we were all hot and tired. The children went to bed, and we listened to music on the record player in the drawing room. This was my first encounter with Sibelius, and I loved the music. "It makes Lisa's Baltic heart beat faster," Bob said while I copied Taqui lying flat on the carpet. That position helped me to enjoy the music. I began to dream of past summer holidays.

On the following morning I offered to cycle down to the village to buy some bread and milk. I found out that British bikes do not brake when pedalled backwards. So there I was, approaching the first bend at great speed and, not very gracefully, somersaulting into the meadow on my left. I had a few bruises and scratches, but bike and shopping bag were all right. So I pushed the bike back uphill, hid it in the garage and walked down to the village on foot; struggling back uphill – with a bag full of milk and bread – was no fun at all.

Taqui and the children had gone ahead to the boathouse while Bob waited, wondering why I had been so long. "Did you not find the first gear for driving uphill?" he wanted to know.

"I did not drive at all", I grumbled. "That bike does not work." While we walked down to the others he explained the intricacies of British bikes, but I never again trusted them.

A Swallow or an Amazon?

We sailed in one boat only, as Taqui had to teach Bob how to sail and me how to use the tiller. There was plenty of room for three adults, two small children, two picnic baskets and Bob's fishing tackle. And again it was a glorious day. Our boat safely entered the small inlet which Taqui's family usually made their harbour. Bob jumped out to tie the rope to a tree, and all of us followed, gathering some picnic items each.

We climbed on a narrow path to a place on top, which the Altounyans had always used as their picnic place: it was a flat rocky area, partly overgrown with soft grass around a charcoal-stained spot in the centre. Down below we could see another inlet, deep water surrounded by large rocks. It was there that we could swim and Bob could sit high up, fishing for something good for our next meal. But before that we had to scramble around the surprisingly large island to collect brushwood. Taqui pointed to some isolated houses in the forest on the opposite shore and also to the area where Arthur Ransome had had his house. When we had enough wood, Bob lit a fire. Taqui opened tins of baked beans, unwrapped sausages, bread, butter and poured drinks into plastic mugs. She had brought a small saucepan and a frying pan, and soon we could smell delicious food.

After the meal we climbed down to the swimming place, both children carrying inflated rings, though Chimpy could almost swim on his own. Bob sat on higher rocks and soon caught an enormous pike, too large to fit into the bucket we had filled with water for that purpose. Bob had to bang its head on the rocks, then gut it for dinner at home. We saw the sunset as our boat gently drifted back towards its house.

One evening Taqui and Bob set off on their own, sailing to our picnic place on Peel Island, where they wanted to spend the night and have dinner and breakfast on their own. I enjoyed Lane Head and its surroundings with the boys. Nicky, not yet two years old and still sometimes wearing nappies, already seemed to be a real boy, sweeter than Chimpy, but not as bright. I loved them both. Bob went back to work in London before we left, and I was pleased when he wrote that he had found the ideal house in Barnes, but that it required a great deal of work. So, could I suggest where I would spend a month with the children? I suggested Aberystwyth, and Bob and Taqui accepted my idea.

I knew that TJ's house would be empty all August, because he was in London, Marlene in Freyersen, and Mrs Porter with her sister. We took the minimum of clothing, but it still seemed too much to carry it – and Nicky – uphill to TJ's house. I was looking for a taxi, when I saw Mr Edwards, the Bath Street Chapel elder. We greeted each other with reciprocal delight and he offered to give us a lift; but he thought I would be better off with his family than all on my own with the children. I was not convinced, but thought it would be rude to refuse such a well-meant offer. Yet: after one week they asked me for lodger's money. It was far more than I could afford with the cash that the Stephens had given me, thinking of food, drink and occasional children's treats only. I had written to Taqui about these kind people who looked after us, giving us breakfast and Sunday lunch and often baby-sitting at night for me. Now I felt too proud to admit to the Stephenses that I had made a mistake. In order to have more money, I simply asked them for it, knowing that they would think I had over-spent my allowance with treats. In fact, I had to deprive Chimpy and Nicky of treats altogether.

In spite of these absurd financial worries our holiday was wonderful. We left for the beach immediately after breakfast and there we met friends of Marlene's who had young children and numerous buckets and spades. Nicky was so charming, he

101

attracted many people we had not been introduced to. I shall never forget how this little man stood on the sands with outstretched hands, a few bread-crumbs on them, calling in a lovely, soft, imploring voice "Seagull birdie, seagull birdie…" and looking puzzled when these birdies circled around him, but did not come to pick the crumbs. It broke my heart to watch his little face, but there was nothing I could do to persuade the gulls that Nicky meant well. Fortunately the curate of the Anglican church near Ifor Evans's house distracted him with nursery rhymes, changing to stories about King Arthur and Sir Galahad for Chimpy, who was pleased to do all the actions for receiving his own knighthood and wielding a stick as his sword. He also heard stories about Guinevere and Sir Lancelot, told from an innocent priest's point of view.

Marlene prepared a farewell meal for us at TJ's house. Many of our new friends came to wave good-bye at the station, and the curate gave me his large white handkerchief to wipe away my tears, which, alas, did not flow. Other friends gave goodies to the children for the long journey. On the train we looked out of the window and Chimpy and I made up stories about the things or people we saw. Nicky slept on my lap.

London again

Bob and Taqui were standing on the platform in Paddington station, and when I told the children that their Mummy and Daddy were there, they began to run towards them, shouting with delight, then, suddenly they made U-turns and ran back to hide their faces in my skirt. Taqui took this as a sign of how they had enjoyed our time together and laughed about it – very different from Tante Eka, who had nearly cried when Heidi hid from her, after her mother had gone to stay with her father in barracks in 1943, and left her and her older brother Eberhard with me at Mickelau for two weeks. Heidi had been only two years old then, just a few months older than Nicky was now.

By the time we set out for the new house in Barnes, the children were already, at first timidly, beginning to cuddle up to their parents.

The impressive house stood in a beautiful situation, right next to Barnes Common. The children rushed around, finding their own rooms, their parents' bedroom and on the highest floor my own room with a spare room next to it. The kitchen faced south, toward the street, while the large dining room faced north, towards the Common. The dining table stood under one of the two windows opposite the two doors, one coming from the hall, the other from the kitchen. In one corner were sofa, coffee table, arm chairs, bookshelves.

Chimpy and I often had serious discussions in this corner. I remember telling him about the meaning of Faust and Mephistopheles, but later I wished I had not explained the latter. I did not want him to think of devils with red faces and horns, so I explained that Goethe meant the devil inside people, urging us to do naughty things. But when Chimpy was beating himself one day like a monk chastising himself in his cell and explained to Bob that he was punishing the devil inside him, I felt awfully embarrassed, as if I were bringing up this child in some strict Roman

Catholic sect. I stammered trying to explain... and paid more attention to the possible consequences of my stories after that.

In most respects our life in Barnes was similar to our life in Berlin, except that we did not have Pohlman or any other car, but relied completely on public transport and our own legs, which prevented us from frequently visiting cinemas or theatres on the spur of the moment.

The occasion which reminded me most of Berlin was an invitation by Charles Reid to the opera. As a music critic he was given a certain number of complimentary tickets, but I found it hard to believe that he received free seats for all of us – Bob, Taqui, Tristan and myself in addition to himself and his wife Louise. Perhaps it was his way of thanking us for looking after him in Berlin. I certainly deserved a medal for my patient interpreting efforts, and the lovely Covent Garden Opera House seemed a fair prize. The three opera houses I knew – Vienna, Berlin, London – are built in similar styles, all with that white baroque exterior and the lush red and gold interior. When Charles took us to the bar during the long interval, most of the ladies drank gin-and-It[16], the men drank whisky and I had a dry sherry. Once again I enjoyed having a drink in decorative surroundings. But I have totally forgotten the name of the opera and the singers. I was probably too occupied admiring the setting.

Another occasion I remember was the visit of the curate from Aberystwyth. I met him on Hammersmith Bridge and could hardly recognize the gentleman. Instead of the casual wear and tanned body in swimming trunks, he was now wearing a dark suit, a bowler hat, and carrying an umbrella, rather like a caricature of Chamberlain. He furtively kissed my cheek before he hailed a taxi to take us to a night-club of his choice. I found the club a little uncanny, like some place in a sinister film, but the meal was good, the waiters exceptionally polite and the music discreet. If there was a performance on the stage, I did not see it. We ate many courses, and between courses I relaxed with a cigarette. It was well after midnight when the curate drove me back to Barnes in a taxi. That was the last time I saw or heard of him.

I don't know who gave us the cat, or if the Stephens bought it, or if it strayed into our house. The children were delighted, but the cat was by no means house-trained. Someone suggested sprinkling pepper along the skirting board. So, when Bob and Taqui had gone out to a party one night, I took all the pepper from our storehouse and sprinkled it. My sense of achievement turned to horror when Taqui told me she had just heard that there was going to be a great pepper shortage and we would have to economize.

Tristan had discovered that a friend from his Oxford days, Arthur Lall, had some important position at the Indian embassy. He lived in London with his wife Susheila and their daughter Tookie – a nickname given to her until she wanted to choose her own name; as far as I know, she kept her nickname. One of Arthur's friends was the press attaché and writer Khushwant Singh, whose wife Kaval was extremely beautiful and frequently invited Tristan and me to her dinner parties. I loved her spicy food, but Tristan was most impressed with silver leaf on puddings, because they had "run out of gold leaf", they said. Khushwant himself invited many

---

[16] It = Italian = red vermouth

103

interesting Indian writers and journalists and once introduced me to a maharaja, who explained to me why he needed four wives: one to arrange political affairs such as the schooling and general welfare of his estates' children, another for his own physical needs, a third to teach his own children and a fourth to arrange the menus in his own household and for his parties. He thought he was lucky to be able to afford them all, because by law he was obliged to provide exactly the same for each wife. And, he said, no one woman could fulfil all those many different needs and he was sure that none was jealous of the others. It made good sense to me, better than those odd love affairs hidden away from wives. The centrepiece of all parties was Khushwant's four-year-old daughter Mala, who flew like a whirlwind from one guest to another. I promised myself that I would call my first daughter Mala. In India it means a garland. Mala's brother Rahul was pleasantly intelligent, but not at all the lively, laughing and shouting creature that his sister was.

In Barnes, Taqui, the children and I went for long walks on the common, sometimes joined for picnics by friends like Cynthia, who lived at the other side of the common. We had to make the best of Chimpy's company, because in March he would be five years old, which meant that he could go to school just after Christmas. I was not looking forward to that.

Sometimes Taqui's brother Roger, a medical student, came to stay with us. He slept in the spare room next to mine and was very quiet and considerate on the few occasions when I had gone upstairs before him. He told us of a needy student who, being examined in practical work, had to deliver a baby and dropped it by mistake, but calmly said to the worried mother "Once is enough" and put the baby in her arms. His presence of mind was acknowledged by the examiner and he passed. Mishaps like this happened in many of Roger's stories. He was good company for all of us.

First Visit to Street Acre

Twice Tristan took the Stephenses and me to Street Acre, the country house he was so proud of. It lay in the village of St Nicholas-at-Wade in East Kent and had been built by his parents as their weekend retreat from the stresses of Whitehall. They had stayed in the village with Molly Bernhard-Smith, who ran an art gallery near Whitehall. She was artistic herself, had many famous artist friends and had been married to a doctor who was even more eccentric than she was. I heard stories of him walking in the marshes, playing his little flute behind a curtain in the Margate caves, and chasing girls. He bought a meteorite in some London shop and hurled it at the window of a local JP who had offended him. Then, rushing to the front door he called excitedly: "Did you see that meteorite coming in? No, don't touch it yet, it may still be hot." So the bureaucrat waited for it to cool. Newspapers began to report the incident. An expert was called in to determine where the stone had originated. Then the truth was discovered and next day the headlines reported 'COUNCIL HOAXED'. He also achieved notoriety by daubing raspberry jam on a statue in the British Museum whose nose had been 'repaired'.

Molly herself was keen on playing charades and had an entire wardrobe full of dressing-up clothes in her Thatched Cottage. Claus once came down from Scotland

and enjoyed the games in Molly's house… or maybe he felt flattered by the attention he received from Molly's two nieces. I loved watching them, but hoped that Claus would not make a fool of himself, as I had once seen him do with Marlene's friend Antje, who visited us in London on her return from South America to Germany. She had learnt Canasta and taught us the game, which became a hot favourite for years.

Molly managed to buy for TJ an acre of land from Streete Farm. Tristan's mother designed the garden and a local builder built the house. The overall scheme and some interior work, such as the blue & white tiles on two fireplaces and a large painted plate to be hung on a wall, were done by Sidney Greenslade, the architect who designed the National Library of Wales. I fell in love with the wonderfully bright house. All the walls were cream, magnolia or other off-white colours, and the woodwork was painted white, except for the surrounds of the drawing-room fireplace, which were of plain, unpainted wood. Many of the fireplace tiles were based on drawings the artist had made in the surrounding area plus the initials of TJ and his wife in the centre, their three children above and on either side of the parents. Next to the parents were the mottoes of the Universities of Wales and Liverpool, where Tristan's mother had studied, and next to these the Welsh dragon and the liver-bird. The bottom line of tiles showed the initials of Molly and of two builders and the architect. South-facing windows in the drawing room and dining room (and two upstairs rooms) gave a good view of the front lawn, surrounded by a neat, small yew hedge. East windows in the kitchen and dining room faced the rose-and-herb garden, west windows looked onto the tennis lawn, no longer in use. That lawn was surrounded by herbaceous borders and trees, beyond which stretched one of the fields of Streete Farm. On the horizon to the west, north and north-east we could see Reculver Towers and the sea.

The fireplace

105

At the back of Street Acre were a drive and a large gate, entrances to a double garage and a porch leading to the kitchen and also through to the rose garden. Behind the house grew numerous sweet cherry trees and further beyond a large orchard with a vegetable / soft fruit garden.

The village church was massive, built in the 12th century. Opposite the church was a quaint little grocers' shop. In Downbarton Road were the school (over 100 years old), the butcher's shop, Molly's Thatched Cottage, a Wesleyan chapel, two farms, various farm cottages. Near the upper end, close to the church stood School House, where the headmistress Miss Tett lived. From School House ran Court Road towards the farm and manor house of the newly arrived Tapp family. The street running East from the church was the main village street with a dilapidated former Jewish convalescent home, a narrow alleyway at the side leading to a cobbler's premises, then a bakery. Two pubs faced each other across the street: 'The Bell' on the southern side was over 400 years old and therefore more acceptable to the Jones family than 'The Sun' opposite, which was only 200 years old. Near 'The Sun' stood the village hall, the building of which had been prompted by Tristan's parents. Not far from this, on the same side, stood the village post office. Opposite the Post Office stood an old forge and the second village grocer's shop.

Suffice it to say that I fell in love with the village at first sight, and though much has changed now, that love remains.

Towards Marriage?

Tristan's London flat in Kilburn was small by comparison, though infinitely better than our single room in Freyersen had been. On entering it one was faced with a corridor and a staircase ahead. On the right of the corridor was a small bedroom, on the left a large sitting-dining-bedroom with a Victorian fireplace with stucco garlands of flowers, which Tristan had painted in watercolours. Against a wall a large bed folded away behind a wishy-washy blue and cream curtain. In front of the bay window stood a folding table and four dining chairs, and near the fireplace was a large, very low cane armchair. There were two or three small bookcases hanging on the wall and that was all.

It was necessary to walk through the communal corridor in order to reach the bedroom from the sitting-room, or from the kitchen further along inside the house for that matter, or from the bathroom upstairs, which was used by all tenants. The bedroom had a large double bed with bedside table and a wardrobe with shelves for underwear and sheets, and table linen or towels along one side. A few rugs made the floor look habitable, just as the sitting-dining room had a large green carpet.

The kitchen was a small room opposite the telephone under the stairs. It had a small cooker, a sink with hot- and cold-water taps, a tiny fridge, a tall, narrow cupboard which was sold to Tristan as a 'broom cupboard', but which he equipped with shelves inside, painting the outside with a long-necked giraffe and other creatures.

Despite the limited appeal of The Avenue, and against all my resolutions not to get married before I was 30, and with all my aversion to divorce, I did, one night, heaven knows why, decide that I would live with Tristan to help him get his divorce from a wife he obviously no longer loved.

When I told Taqui of my decision, she did not even appear surprised. I said I would stay with them until they had found another mother's help and in a way I hoped that they never would. But they did, at least on a temporary basis: Taqui's aunt, who lived in France had been a close friend of a pianist lady, who had a daughter called Gisèle Aton. This girl was coming to London with a tourist visa for three weeks. Her real wish was to sell her designs for dress materials, but she liked the idea of staying with the Stephens family. So I cleared out my room for her and introduced her to most of the tasks she would be expected to do. She immediately fell in love with sweet Nicky, but found Chimpy rather a spoilt brat. I was annoyed, but as I wanted her to stay and thought that Chimpy was nearly old enough to cope, I did not show my anger.

Meanwhile Tristan had been sent to Munich by the Observer in a chauffeur-driven car. He dropped in on Edith, who had gone back to university after our time with the News Guardian. She now lived in Münster, and her best friend at university had just lost her fiancé in an accident. Apparently he had been a talented man, called "the future Hemingway" by some. So Edith thought it would be a good idea for Hella to travel to Munich with Tristan. Tristan was only too willing to oblige, because the girl was attractive and, he told me, "kind enough to allow me to put my hand on her knee." He probably said that to make me jealous, and he succeeded. Nevertheless I asked if she might find it a distraction from her grief, if she came to London after Gisèle had to leave for France again. So Tristan and Edith arranged for Hella to come to the Stephenses.

Meanwhile Gisèle had fallen in love with Taqui's brother and more or less told him so. But Roger said that his father was so anti-French that he could not confront him with a prospective French wife. The girl bowed to fate and, having tried unsuccessfully to sell her material designs to big shops like Liberty's, returned to Paris after a brief trip to Street Acre with me. She, too, loved "our" house.

Before Hella arrived, Tristan and Roger thought up a trick to play on her, one that was typical for both men: they put a vacuum cleaner under Hella's bed and led the flex carefully along the wall into Roger's room where he would turn it on as soon as he could hear through the wall that Hella was going to bed. Unfortunately she was still so used to students' life that she went to bed very late and Tristan and I could not wait for her shriek, because we needed to catch the last bus. So we only heard next morning that the trick had worked. It evidently did not put her off Roger, however, as she ended up marrying him – which casts a strange light on his father's prejudice.

On 17 December 1949 I officially moved into The Avenue, Kilburn and began to call myself Mrs Jones. I consider that day my real wedding day and cannot remember the legal date.

Taqui still kept urging me to write my memoirs of our days on the open road before I became bogged down with children and housework. She herself had always wanted to write, but had never yet managed it. So she gave me Eliot's 'Four Quartets' as a Christmas present and marked the passage which begins: 'So here I am, in the middle way, having had twenty years – Twenty years largely wasted, the years of *l'entre deux guerres* – Trying to learn to use words, and every attempt is a wholly new start, a different kind of failure…' I had tried starting to write when I was TJ's housekeeper, giving up again and again. Unlike Taqui, I knew I was not cut out to be a writer.

We spent the Christmas season with the Obanks. Ken came to fetch us in his car and in a proper London pea-soup fog. I had never experienced anything like it. It was frightening to feel our way through Bushy Park and towards Teddington. We took so long that Ken's wife Mary and the two children were becoming worried. We arrived just in time to see 'The Wind in the Willows' on television. Tristan had read the story to me long ago, but these creatures were not in the least the ones I had imagined. Hollywood at its worst, or television at its worst? When TJ was given a television by David Astor who — rightly — thought it would keep him company, TJ said "O God! Have I come to that? Just pre-digested food?" So the well-meaning Obanks were failing in their attempts to give me a lovely Christmas. But the plum pudding was some compensation. Most German people hate English plum puddings, but I loved them then and still do.

Mary Obank asked if I could get her a mother's help in Germany. I thought my cousin Ilse might be interested. She had trained to be a nurse and came almost by return post.

A month later Ken and Tristan had to go to Germany on Servob business and took Ilse and me with them to visit our families. Ilse was so anxious to speak English that at the German customs she could only think of the few English words she knew in reply. One of the men asked me in German, "Could you please translate for this lady?" Both Ilse and I felt embarrassed. When we had safely gone through the customs, Tristan noticed that there was a packet of tea we had not declared. So he grabbed it and threw it to the surprised customs officer. We others were furious.

I did not tell the Brinkmanns that I had decided to live with, i.e. marry Tristan, thinking they would be too religious to accept marriage to a divorced man.

After a few days with our families the men came to pick us up again. By that time I realized that I was pregnant and hoped nobody would notice. There were still seven months to go, and the pregnancy might make Tristan's wife Mary opt for divorce. Eirene later said that ours was the worst strategy towards Mary, who had always badly wanted a family and whose wish had been ignored by Tristan. He said, even to me, that he would make a bad father, but trusted me to fulfil the roles of both father and mother, unlike Mary.

That summer, even though I was no longer their mother's help, the Stephenses asked if I would join them for a Coniston holiday again. This time we would not be able to stay in Lanehead. By now both Taqui's parents had died and had left Lanehead to Titty, who was either living there with her large family or had sold the house. Whatever the case, we were going to live in a house that belonged to one of Taqui's aunts and was called The Barn. The house was small, but very pleasant and light. It did look out on to Lake Coniston. This time we took Bob's sister's children, Bobby and Jane with us. Every day they sang "Put another nickel in, in the Nickelodeon."

Taqui still had access to the two sailing boats and, while she took the four children with her, she believed Bob to be trained enough to take responsibility for

8-months-pregnant me. Bob found the prospect daunting, but managed very well and I again felt spoilt and happy. This year the rain and umbrella postcards made sense. But we were all prepared with raincoats and indoor games.

Picnic on Peel Island

Our baby should have been born on 27 September as an 80th birthday present for TJ, but it made us wait for a few days. Then, as I was coming downstairs from our communal bathroom, I suddenly felt water pouring out of me and called for help. Tristan came and phoned the hospital, which sent an ambulance. But unfortunately, as there was no water left inside me to wash the baby out, I spent 36 hours in labour. Only then was I taken to the labour ward, where I was told off when I pleaded for a Caesarean or something to warrant a full anaesthetic. Eventually they took the baby out with forceps and I fell asleep. Next morning I was told that my baby boy was suffering from birth shock and could not yet be brought to me. (Tristan later told me that they did not want me to see how squashed his head looked.)

When Tristan came to see me in the morning, bringing a bunch of flowers as usual, he talked of having seen 'The Third Man' with Ilse in the local cinema and bought a record of the Harry Lime Theme for me to hear when I came home. I began to wonder if something terrible had happened to our baby, because he did not mention it at all. So I asked him what he thought of the baby. "What baby?" he asked. Nobody had told him, and he stormed out to the nursery. When he came back he looked very happy. "He is beautiful. You will be able to feed him tomorrow." Meanwhile we had to think of a name, as we could hardly call him

Mala. Tristan said "As he is our first man, he should really be called Adam. Besides, Adam von Trott was such a good man – but I had better consult David (Astor) first."

A rare photo of the 'man of a thousand secrets' relaxing

»Vater«, sprach sie, »wie oft gedachten wir, untereinander schwatzend, des fröhlichen Tags, der kommen würde, wenn künftig Hermann, seine Braut sich erwählend, uns endlich erfreute! Hin und wider dachten wir da; bald dieses, bald jenes Mädchen bestimmten wir ihm mit elterlichem Geschwätze. Nun ist er kommen, der Tag; nun hat die Braut ihm der Himmel hergeführt.« [...] Da stand der Geistliche schnell auf, nahm das Wort und sprach: »Der Augenblick nur entscheidet über das Leben des Menschen und über sein ganzes Geschicke; denn nach langer Beratung ist doch ein jeder Entschluß nur Werk des Moments, es ergreift doch nur der Veränd'ge das Rechte. Immer gefährlicher ist's, beim Wählen dieses und jenes Nebenher zu bedenken und so das Gefühl zu verwirren.«

"Father," she said, "how oft, in our idle chatter, did we think of the joyful day to come when Hermann would make us happy by selecting his bride? Again and again we thought 'is this the one?' 'is that the one?', choosing for him with our parental prattle. Now the day has come; now heaven has brought him his bride." [...] The priest then leapt to his feet and spoke: "Our lives, our fates, are decided only in the instant; even after long deliberation, matters are determined in a mere moment, wise people simply seize the sensible options. Examining extra considerations in a choice confuses one's instincts, and therein lies danger."

Goethe (Hermann und Dorothea)

111

Wedding photo, August 1951
The witnesses were Taqui & Bob Stephens, Sybil Jerome and Khushwant Singh

11. I hereby apply to be registered as a citizen of the United Kingdom and Colonies.

I, *ANNELIESE CHARLOTTE FRIEDA JONES*
do solemnly and sincerely declare that the foregoing particulars stated in this application are true, and I make this solemn declaration conscientiously believing the same to be true.

(Signature of applicant)... *Anneliese Jones*

Made and subscribed this... *7th*... day of... *September*... 195*1*

Application for naturalization, September 1951

Family life

Over the next 35 years, my life was almost entirely occupied with bringing up the family – daily routines during term time, then enjoyable holidays where I was able to introduce them to the delights of walking in the mountains near Salzburg, combined with exposure to top-class music. I'd always dreamed of them playing music together, and even took up the viola and recorder myself to encourage this, although they soon outstripped my meagre abilities.

Our home was no farm, but it was rural and full of animals – just the one horse, but also a donkey (Mumbo Jumbo), goat (Seth), geese, chickens, a duck, countless dogs (including Hennessey Tennessee Supremacy), and a peacock (Henry). He was my favourite as he was free to leave but chose to stay with us, although he did steal rusks from the children's pram; Ben's first words were "Henry, get down!". The menagerie meant that we acquired quite a reputation, and if the RSPCA rescued an unusual animal they would often house it with us – I remember a guillemot, four huge St Bernards, and numerous foxes, some of whom became so tame they could be taken to Canterbury on the bus. The village school once sent back a note saying that our children had to learn not to embellish stories about their 'pets', and I had to inform them that in fact there was no exaggeration.

King Henry and his subjects

Despite being the only foreigner in St Nicholas-at-Wade, I made sure our children had every opportunity to mix with others of all backgrounds, taking large groups of them on trips to the beach most days in the summer. The local trampoline operator at Reculver even came to refer to me as "Mrs Christmas", which I found quite funny. Sometimes we would also go to the Ernest Read children's concerts in London, combined with a visit to the Science Museum or Natural History Museum, and of course a picnic somewhere too. Following in my father's footsteps, I made some screens so that our attic functioned as a darkroom, where our photography club developed black and white photographs of each other, then cut them into collages or drew on glass above the photographs to create strange effects. I also tried to understand the village by researching and documenting its history, producing a limited edition 'book' at the time of the Silver Jubilee, as well as a 'census' full of useless but (to my mind) interesting information such as the ratio of pets to humans in each street! Thinking back now, perhaps this was driven by my knowledge of how easy it was for even idyllic rural communities to be lost.

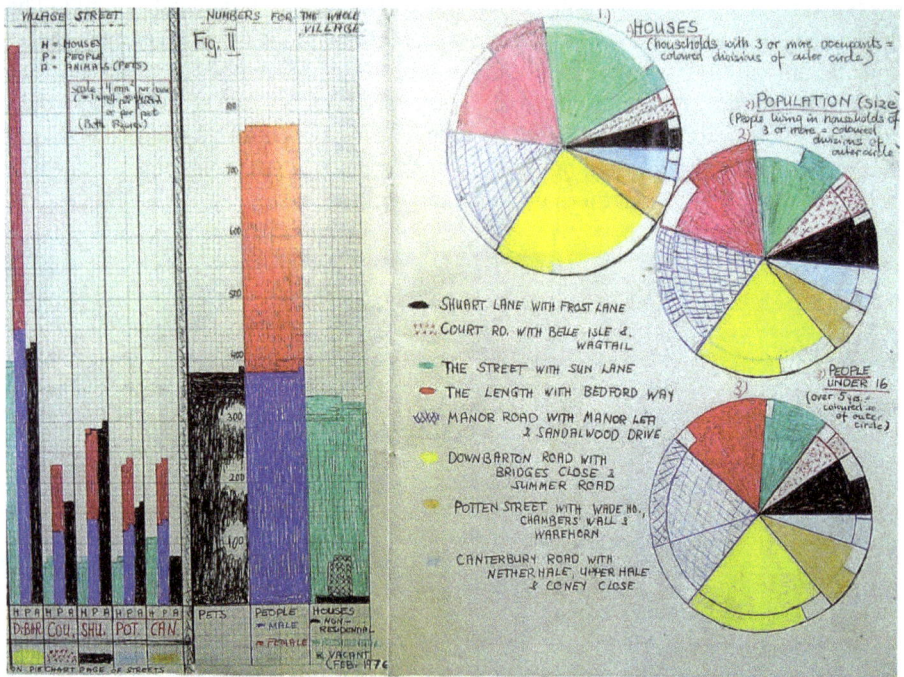

Part of my village census

Tristan's friendship with David Astor meant that we would regularly visit Cliveden on Observer outings, although this was a decade after the "Cliveden set" (many of whom TJ knew) and some years before the Profumo affair. I recall Adam and Mala conducting the band of Welsh Guards in front of the grand staircase in 1954, and Chimpy exclaiming "I bet The Times take their staff for a miserly walk on Hampstead Heath!" Jane Bown took some pictures of the children on the Astor slides, switch-backs, climbing frames and their boat on the Thames, and I heard that even complete strangers had ordered some of them.

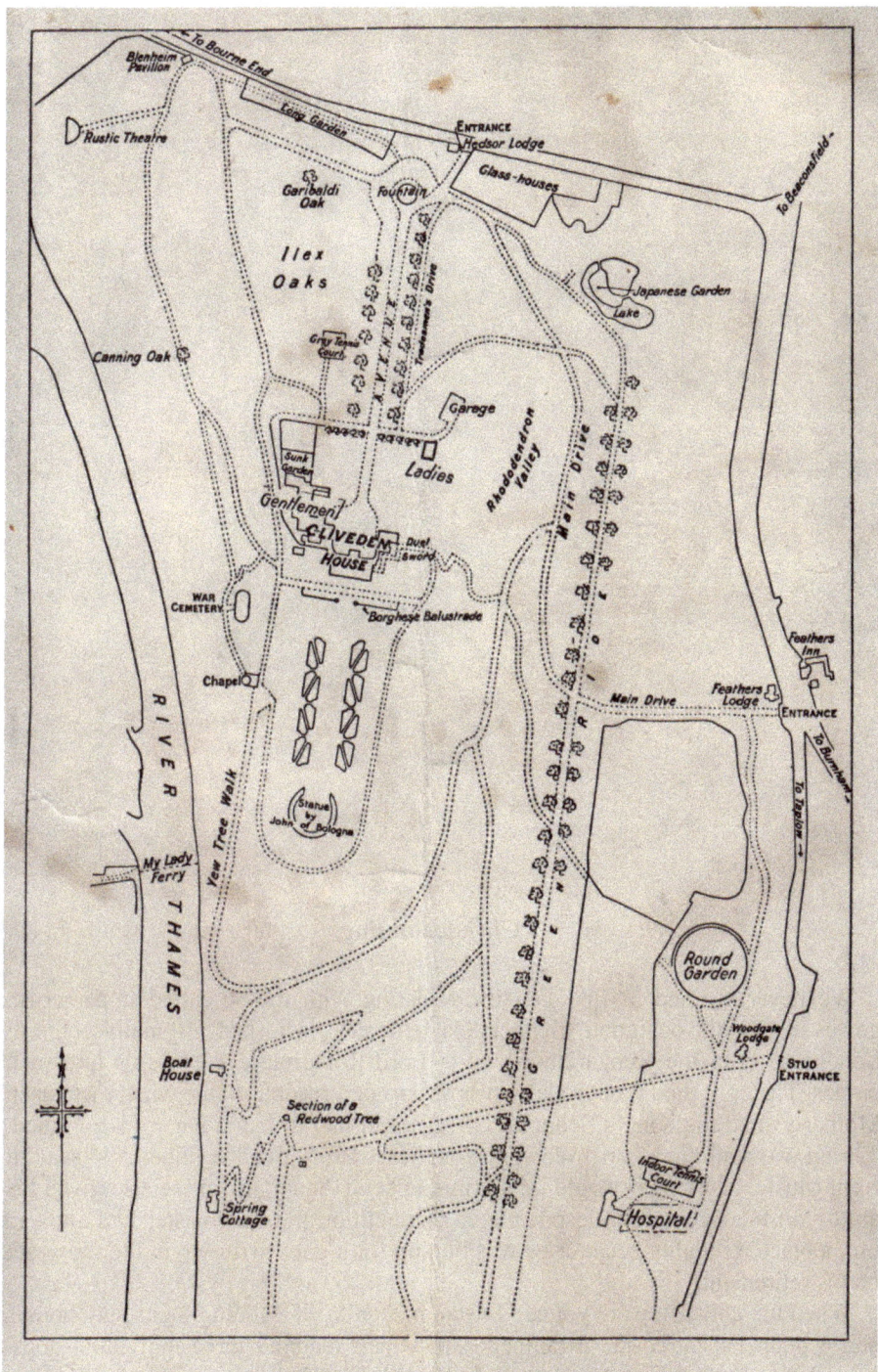

Map of Cliveden

Cliveden outing

We never seemed to find David circulating with the so-called upper crust, however, nor did our good friend Lajos Léderer[17], who had originally come to London to offer the Hungarian crown to Lord Rothermere, elevate us into such circles. The only time I met royalty was as part of a reception line when the Queen Mother visited the King's School in 1962, and I had to buy a hat, which I hated. Tristan was again in a borrowed suit, from Moss Bros. Yvonne Enoch, the head of Kent Music, had said it would be a crime to send Adam anywhere else given his ability on the violin, and despite fierce competition the headmaster had allowed him a place, probably because he was hoping for a good write-up in the Observer on his retirement.

When the children were young, Tristan had enjoyed building them play houses and a puppet theatre, and a ramped barn which featured three individual dogs' kennels on the first floor, opened and closed by pulleys from below, but he later developed heart problems and was advised to abandon carpentry as a hobby. David

---

[17] Observer correspondent for Eastern Europe.

gave Tristan a cine camera as an alternative pastime, but he showed little interest, and spent most of his free time collecting commemorative ceramics and treen. I then borrowed his device to make silent adventure films starring our children, who had by then increased to four, and their many friends from the village school. It is only much later that we discovered a letter by Tristan saying that he had taken up collecting because he was unable to get life insurance, and wanted to provide for his family.

We similarly gave up on joint family holidays, after one disastrous attempt. A few years after the war, the German government had instituted a scheme called *Lastenausgleich* to compensate those who had lost their East Prussian estates, and fortunately we had taken our farm registers with us on the trek, which proved what kind of property we had, how many people had been employed there, and so on. When Omi, Marlene and I received our payments, we first shared them with Claus, who did not qualify, having been in Scotland on the specific date used – although he was given free tenancy of a small farm. I then decided I wanted to blow all of mine on one luxurious, memorable holiday.

We first had a couple of days at Hahnenklee in the Harz mountains, then drove towards the Rhine, although Tristan kept leapfrogging a Mercedes on the Autobahn to demonstrate that his car was faster, and Mala consequently kept being sick. We inspected a wine cellar, dined on wild boar, saw some important monuments and visited museums… and the children were bored stiff. I vowed that would be the last time, although we did many years later take our fifth child on a road trip to Wales. He too was sick, into a policeman's helmet. On this trip I would sometimes leave Tristan in the antique shops and walk the hills, although strangely never coming closer to "Llwybr Cyhoeddus", which I assumed was a large town. It was only later I discovered this to mean "public footpath".

I did take the children to various parts of Germany and Austria myself, once every two years, and visited several relatives: although Marlene had also settled in the UK, Mutti, Omi and Claus were living near Bremen, with other family members and friends 'from back home' quite close. As the children grew, we went on holiday also behind the Iron Curtain, to Czechoslovakia in 1971 and Hungary in 1981. East Prussia itself, however, remained resolutely out of bounds, as it was now part of Russia – to be precise, an exclave called Kaliningradskaya Oblast – and to cap it all, contained military facilities. Russia's acquisition of Königsberg at the Potsdam Conference had given it an ice-free port in the Baltic, so the Soviet Baltic Fleet was based there for much of the Cold War, and with several air bases nearby, the area was said to be the most heavily militarized in Europe. Furthermore, its location at the westernmost tip of Russia meant it was regarded as a prime location for stationing missiles.

Greenham Common

I had no love for war, whatever the pretext. When I discovered in 1981 that our government had stolen land that had been used for their recreation from the people of Greenham, I felt angry about the theft and, worse still, about the way this stolen land was given to the Americans to build huge silos to house their cruise missiles.

And when I was told that coaches were leaving from Canterbury to take protesters to Greenham Common, I quickly applied for a place.

It was a truly great day: hundreds of coaches, thousands of people, tying protest messages to the high wire mesh fence, shouting in anger and singing peace songs such as "Where have all the flowers gone?" and "Deus donna nobis pacem", along with stirring tunes like "John Brown's body" or "We shall not be moved". The Observer had written a very favourable article about the CND crowds arriving and the paper was handed to us for free. I felt so moved, I nearly cried.

Of course, there were also some silly aspects, such as women saying "Hold hands to feel the force" (which I did not feel) and similar remarks. However, we did hold hands and managed to surround all those 17 miles of the fence in a circle of peace banners – while above us an Olga Maitland aeroplane trailed a long banner, giving us the Kremlin's greetings and gratitude.

At dusk we sat around the fence, lighting the candles we had brought along and enjoying our different picnic meals. Some good voices sang lovely soprano peace songs. It was all so wonderfully moving, and I decided to join Canterbury CND on our return journey. Several months later I joined National CND. Having successfully avoided the Hitler Youth, this was the first time for me to join a party – of the political kind.

Molesworth Peace Camp
Portakabin police patrolling our placards, doves and rainbows across the razor wire

Marlene had long been involved in the peace movement, and we frequently met up at rallies in London or protests at military bases. Our status as former war refugees, and above all Germans who were against all militarism, seemed to go down well with the Aldermaston anarchists and others we met; conversely, when we attended an event in Germany shortly after the Falklands War, I remember some

118

locals being very wary of our GB numberplate. Marlene was more of an activist than me, and even went to prison as a result.

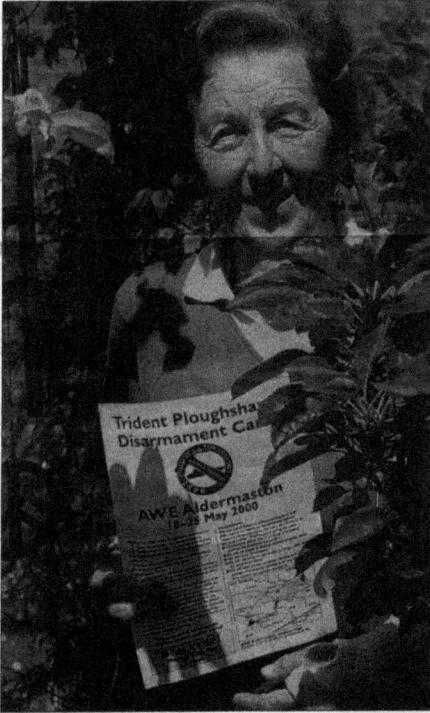

Leicester Mercury

www.thisisleicestershire.co.uk   THURSDAY, JUNE 1, 2000   27p

PLEDGE: ANTI-NUCLEAR CAMPAIGNER WILL NOT PAY BILL FOR FENCE DAMAGE

GRAN, 69, PREPARED FOR JAIL

A 69-year-old grandmother says she will go to prison rather than pay £291, her share of a bill to repair damaged fencing at the Atomic Weapons Establishment in Aldermaston.

Marlene Yeo of Burton-on-the-Wolds, near Loughborough, said: "I helped cut the fence so we could reach people inside to try and convince them they shouldn't be working there.

"I have been campaigning against nuclear weapons for nearly 30 years and will continue to do so.

"I will go to prison rather than pay the damages.

BY JIM McPHEATOR

"I am not looking forward to that but I have the support of my husband and three children.

"I am effectively campaigning for the future of my three grandchildren."

Mrs Yeo was convicted by magistrates in March of criminal damage.

She and her three co-defendants were ordered to pay for repairs to the perimeter fencing at the Berkshire establishment.

Mrs Yeo appeared before Loughborough Magistrates' Court on May 22 for non payment of £250 court costs and the £291 damages.

Magistrates adjourned the hearing until July 3 saying they wanted to seek information from the Ministry of Defence.

Since then Mrs Yeo has written to the court enclosing a cheque for the £250 costs.

But in an accompanying letter, a copy of which she supplied to the Mercury she states: "I do not intend to pay the repair costs.

AWE Aldermaston manufac-

"I will go to prison rather than pay the damages. I am not looking forward to that but I have the support of my husband and three children."
Marlene Yeo

tures the nuclear warheads that are used by the British Trident Nuclear Submarines, and which are so destructive as to be incompatible with international and British laws of warfare.

"They also are a constant danger to the population and environment because of the risk of accidents."

She adds: "I believe I was justified in committing this damage."

She added: "However, as the court hearing did, at least, give me an opportunity of putting forward my arguments, I am willing to pay my share of the court costs."

MAKING A STAND: Protester Marlene Yeo says that she is prepared to face a term in prison

Marlene goes to jail

A different kind of party

Later I became interested in the Green Party and offered them the use of our tool shed gable, which had once hosted a huge portrait of Harold Wilson and was easily visible from St Nicholas roundabout. But the Green Party did not have the money for printing huge posters. So I visited meetings instead.

These were chaired by Jonathan Porritt, who was a modest, sensible man with a quiet voice. Mrs Williams, in whose house we met, offered us cups of tea and biscuits while we talked and planned strategies for the next election. Porritt was not charismatic, but pleasant. I was most impressed with the energy of Lucy Williams (our host's daughter) who was studying for her PhD at Kent University.

Somebody suggested we would collect newspapers for recycling with a firm who paid us some money for each lorryload of paper. It was probably crazy, as we spent more on petrol when taking papers to that lorry than we were paid for a full load, but it felt good to try. Most Green Party members were strict vegetarians and enjoyed exploring our vegetable garden, which at its peak contained 57 different varieties.

In several cases our social meetings led to marriages. I attended a reception in a Preston pub and another in the 'Friends Meeting House' in Canterbury because the couple were both Quakers and had a Quaker ceremony. David and Louise asked if they could have their reception in our barn and a children's entertainer on the patio outside the barn. Everybody contributed food and drink to that wedding reception and the numerous children enjoyed their entertainer's puppet show. Hundreds of green balloons decorated our garden – to my mind, the best type of party. My grandson later even nicknamed me 'partyholic'.

We had much fun in general, but when someone asked me if I were willing to stand as a "paper candidate" for the imminent council elections, I lost the feeling of fun. I agreed that my name could go on to ballot papers for 'Birchington and Villages', but I certainly refused to canvas for myself. I distributed leaflets for Will Jarman, who stood for the Westgate Ward as a serious contender (not a paper candidate as I was).

Nevertheless, when it came to the count, I discovered that exactly a thousand people had voted for me, neither 999, nor 1001, but exactly 1000! Fortunately my Tory opponent had more than twice as many votes, so there was no danger of myself going to council meetings, or even to give an acceptance speech! I am certainly not a public speaker. But it was gratifying to hear Mr Fox say in his acceptance speech that my relative success had taught him to take some green ideas on board, even if others accused him of hijacking our agenda. Apparently my result – despite, or possibly thanks to, the lack of effort on my part – was the highest the Greens ever scored in Thanet.

I decided to leave the Green Party a few years later, when my heroine Petra Kelly and her boyfriend, the ex-general Gert Bastian, committed suicide (as it was reported at the time). I remained a member of CND, but never again joined a political party... which does not mean that I lost my interest in politics! Far from it, I still read as many papers as I can and listen to most of the party political broadcasts. I admired Michael Foot and Shirley Williams (but not David Owen or Bill Rodgers), Betty Boothroyd, and several foreign politicians such as Nelson Mandela – and Ghandi, of course – as well as many non-political men like the late David Astor. I continued to attend many political events, such as those organized by Marlene and her husband Peter for the Golden Oldies Against Trident (GOATs), until I lost mobility by breaking my right hip following a hoodening party. As a consequence, my youngest son named me the 'Revolting Granny', a title which I found rather rude, but funny at the same time.

Rebel and grandmother Anneli joins protesters against war

On December 16, more than 80 protesters blocked the gates of Faslane nuclear base near Glasgow for several hours.
Among them was a spritely grandmother from Thanet whose hatred of war began when she grew up in Hitler's Germany.
Anneli Jones, 84, told EILEEN O'BRIEN why on February 24 she will be protesting again against Trident and troops in Iraq at a rally in Trafalgar Square London.

A life less ordinary: Anti-nuclear protester 84-year-old Anneli Jones from St Nicholas.   thvnr220107anneli-1

ANNELI Jones of St Nicholas is talking about her five children who went to the village school and her five grandchildren.

"It is the prospect of their and their generation's future that frightens me into political protests and joining the blockade at Faslane.

"I've been carrying 'not in my name' banners against troops in Iraq for a long time and was part of the protest rally that knocked down an effigy of Bush in Trafalgar Square like the Americans knocked down an effigy of Saddam Hussein."

It is hard for Anneli to pinpoint exactly what prompted her hatred of war.

"I've always been anti-war. I can't remember a time when I wasn't," she muses, but it is not difficult to see how her childhood, on a farm in Kaliningradskaya Oblast, then in north-eastern Germany and now part of Russia, would have pushed her towards that view.

She was 16 when war broke out and saw many "nasty experiences" living under Nazi rule, even having to take to the road in an open horse-drawn carriage for four months to escape questioning.

Anneli had unwittingly drawn attention to herself after asking a Czech translator at the Slavonic Institute to read a letter from a Ukrainian slave worker.

She recalls: "I was so naive. I even tried to join the Czech resistance but they wouldn't have me.

"They didn't trust me I suppose. I've always been a rebel and always had strong ideas."

In 1942, Anneli went to university in Vienna and later Prague to study journalism, history and German literature.

It led to a job in the British quarter of western Berlin for the foreign correspondent of London's Observer newspaper.

After a year, in 1948, the Russians closed the borders and the Cold War between the Soviet Union and the West began.

Anneli was evacuated to London where she met the man who was to become her husband, Observer journalist Tristan Jones, who later became the paper's managing director.

In 1950, with baby son Adam, now 56, they moved to Stuart Lane, St Nicholas. Children Mala, now 54, and Sarah-Bronwyn, now 49, Goronwy, now 52, and Ben, now 40, followed, which put her activities as a peace campaigner on the back burner.

In 1981, when ground-launched cruise missiles arrived at RAF Greenham Common airbase near Newbury, Berkshire, Anneli took action.

Before long she was a regular protester and an avid CND campaigner.

She took part in rallies, sometimes with her sister Marlena, an even more rebellious campaigner who has been imprisoned for her beliefs.

Anneli's main efforts now are supporting a group set up by Marlena's husband Peter Yeo.

Golden Oldies Against Trident (Goat) is a group of older supporters of the Trident Ploughshares campaign to disarm the UK of Trident nuclear weapons.

She said: "I want Britain to set a good example and get rid of her nuclear weapons.

"Although I am 84 I feel like a spring chicken compared with our 94-year-old protester Alison Beer from the Midlands who comes to rallies in her wheelchair."

After outwitting Nazi authorities, Anneli takes no prisoners in her pursuit of peace.

She takes five-mile protest marches in her stride and will not be put off by government officials in her path.

"At the moment I'm making submissions to the Defence Committee - a parliamentary inquiry into the feasibility of updating Trident weapons – in the hope of introducing at least some doubts among those who might still believe that grand arms deter, rather than encourage terrorists."

The CND demonstration on February 24 that Anneli will be attending assembles at noon at Speaker's Corner in Hyde Park and makes its way to a rally in Trafalgar Square.

For further information about CND visit www.cnduk.org, Stop the War coalition www.stopwar.org.uk trident plough shares.org.

Campaigner: Anneli with members of Goat (Golden Oldies Against Trident).   them230107protest-1

> Although I am 84 I feel like a spring chicken compared with our 94-year-old protester Alison Beer...

'Revolting Granny'

Another day to seize

The first of our children to get married presented another excuse to be creative, eccentric, or classy, depending on the views of the various people involved. At the Observer, Tristan had once noticed an advertisement for a "state coach, bought in error, quick sale preferred". He was already interested in carriages, so intrigued by how anyone could buy such a thing 'in error' he called the seller. Apparently they had been at an auction intending to bid on Lot 16, a Stage Coach, but dozed off and mistakenly bought Lot 17, a State Coach – in fact one that had been used as a town coach by George IV and come from the Royal Mews. When selling it off, the palace had removed all royal coats of arms from the sides, but if one removed the wheels and scraped the grease off the axles, the embossed G IV R moniker was still visible.

A few of the coaches at Street Acre

To someone of my husband's temperament it was naturally tempting, but the seller said that three others had already expressed an interest and were coming to view it the next day. Tristan said "give me ten minutes", then called back and said "OK, I'll buy it – without viewing. £400.". He then stored it in a local farmer's barn, before having it delivered to Street Acre by tractor on Christmas morning as a surprise present. He also commissioned a coach painter to reinstate the side motifs and coloured lines, which needed to be applied using a special camel-hair brush, as used on Rolls Royce cars and the like. Fortunately, when the painter raised the external shutter windows, they discovered the original colours were still visible: someone had forgotten to remove them originally, and when the coach was used in the film The Scarlet Pimpernel, they had not even realized there were two layers of window, operated by different sashes.

The Royal Coach

Visitors to Street Acre were offered a chance to sit in this coach, along with explanations of the construction, and the symbolism in the embroidery. But it was basically locked in a shed most of the time, behind some 'Folly' doors, so any opportunity to use it on the open road had to be grasped. Mala's husband had worried me at first, particularly when Ben said in awe "he drives like Starsky and Hutch!", but we grew to be best friends, and he gamely declared he was willing to have a 'period' wedding, with everyone dressed in Regency costume to match the coach. 'Everyone' meant not just the family, but guests too – including many of the crowds who turned out in the village. Tristan himself wore a viscount's coronet he had acquired from some antique shop, which made a change from the tea cosy he sometimes put on when visiting the local supermarket.

Kind hearts & coronets

It was beautiful to have music for the service provided partly by our children, but also by Clarence Myerscough – the virtuoso violinist who taught Adam and Ben – and his equally talented children Nadia and Lucian, the whole family of course dressed in the appropriate style. Clarence was so down to earth, a pupil who hadn't practised could often distract him into talking about random topics like yoga, beards and antiques… but I did feel outclassed when I mentioned loving fondue with cheddar and white wine, and he said he preferred camembert and champagne. And although Tristan had the proverbial two left feet, I relished the opportunity to spend the evening dancing again – be it Strauss, be it Square Dancing, it is simply indispensable to a proper party.

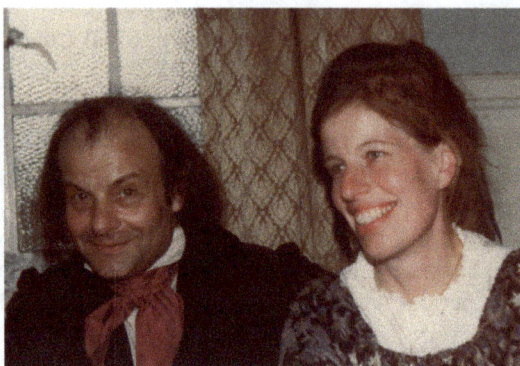

Lucian, Clarence & Marliese

Reunions

Thanks to Claussin, I had remained in touch with Lucien Lebrun, another POW from Mikalbude, who lived in the same Belgian village. We exchanged letters regularly, and he came to visit us in Street Acre in 1982 – exactly on my birthday. This coincided with visits by Mutti, and Marlene and her family, and was a joyful reunion – Mutti was quite thrilled to see him again, and we went to visit Leeds Castle together. I did however also sense that Lucien still had romantic thoughts towards me – war does strange things to people. His own wife had died two years earlier, and he had recently written some memoirs of his wartime experience, « Mes grandes vacances à l'Est », although he seemed reluctant to share them with me.[18] He brought two charming grandchildren on another visit later that year. The strangest development, however, came a decade later when he telephoned, heard that my husband had died, and on the spot switched from « vous » to « tu », saying « Je t'aime beaucoup »… He definitely wanted a relationship! But I found it rather uncanny, and put him off.

---

[18] The memoirs were first shared with Anneli's family ten years after her death.

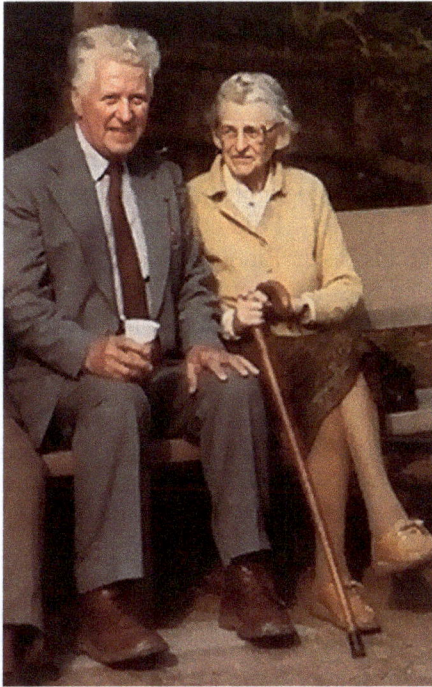
Lucien Lebrun with Mutti at Street Acre, 8 May 1982

There was another unfortunate misunderstanding with the Claussin family. Armand himself had been working as a forestry official, and died on his 71st birthday, 11 June 1987, less than 50 km from where he had been born. I had remained in touch with his daughter, and once wrote that I hoped she would visit, but when she responded with "Thank you for the invitation! I will need some official papers to move to England," I had to disillusion her, and she was so disappointed that she joined a convent.

Meanwhile, Gorbachëv's glasnost and perestroika policies had led to a thawing of the Cold War, and certain limited movement became possible between East Germany and the West. When in 1988 I celebrated my 65th birthday, family and friends past and present assembled, including of course the Stephenses and Gisèle, the Astors, but also my East German cousins Heide (whom I'd last seen in a pram), Gudrun (last seen at Claus's confirmation) and Jutta – on her first trip across the Iron Curtain. We were her closest relatives, but the bloodline had not been judged close enough to allow her to attend Mutti's 80th birthday. But since February 1986, the criterion "urgent family business" had been relaxed in an attempt to relieve the discontent building inside East Germany, and although Jutta still needed to provide official documents to demonstrate that this was a genuine milestone birthday, she was granted the permit to travel. She was most impressed by baked beans, which in her hesitant English she described as 'bones *(Bohnen)* with ketchup'.

Foreign lands

The only 'sports' I have ever enjoyed have been individual ones, practised non-competitively out in nature – horse riding, swimming, ice skating, and above all walking, especially in mountains. Walking around a new country and exploring different cultures was always a delight for me, but while I was bringing up the family – or looking after Tristan – I did not dare to travel for myself. Despite the high regard he had for his sister Eirene and all she had achieved, I knew he considered that my place was at home, while his role was to be the provider. It could be terribly frustrating, and once I even emptied a whole saucepan of soup over his head to drive home how unreasonable he was.

But towards the end of his life, after he had had repeated health problems, our children insisted that I was entitled to a break, and so it was that my life-long wish to see Siberia was fulfilled. I had dreamed so much of bitterly cold snowfields, bears, and wild woods full of howling wolves, that it was a great disappointment to be told the first tour I tried to book had been cancelled due to lack of demand. They offered a similar package for April 1989, and although it was second-best, I snapped up what was available and set off with my middle son Goronwy.

We flew first to Moscow – delayed because of some missing passengers, then a missing tour guide in Moscow, so we only arrived at the Hotel Cosmos after midnight. The next morning, after some wonderful pancake buns with salami and sour cream, accompanied by raspberry juice, our group of thirteen were shown around Red Square, where some bought dolls from black market beggars, then we wandered independently to the ВДНХ Park, far simpler than its official title, the Exhibition of Achievements of the National Economy. Standing amid some soldiers in greatcoats and fur hats – although I felt it almost unbearably hot – we watched some street theatre and lovely, lively dancers I suspected were from Ukraine. The following day we made the giant leap to the east, passing through so many time zones that I ended up totally confused: my diary recalls supper at 00:30 then breakfast at 03:30, sunrise at 01:30 and arrival 05:00 Moscow time, although locally in Khabarovsk it was noon. There I waved in the general direction of my youngest son, now 'only' a few hundred miles away in Japan, and walked around watching pack ice and drunken sailors. I finally plucked up courage to ask some people if they minded me taking their photograph, and had a funny conversation about why my husband was not there, and how far he was from Birmingham. Despite our jet lag, we endured the lectures about war heroes, economic heroes and cultural heroes, then finally managed to join the Trans-Siberian Express, although my hand luggage had meanwhile been stolen. At least I still had some cigarettes, and when I gave a pack to the guard he showered us with gifts of tinned fish and bread.

Then at long last, I could sit and watch the scenery I had dreamed of – wild taiga, broad plains, frozen rivers, huge herds of horses, beautiful sunrises. No photograph could do justice to them, and I was worried because every X-ray machine we'd been through said "not safe for films", but I still snapped away even from inside the train, until I realized my first film had already finished. The sounds too, if only I had thought to bring a cassette recorder! Everywhere we stopped, I heard birds, steamers or tugs hooting, bells and chanting from churches of various denominations, and in between glorious silence across the ice. We were also taken to visit one kindergarten, where delightful giggly children sang a Scottish song for us and showed off their swimming prowess. Now and again we were also treated to some true arctic conditions, although the buildings were always too hot.

After three days on the express, we transferred again to an aeroplane, and gazed out over wide expanses of desolate swamps, before that changed to a cloudscape. Back in Moscow, my 'stolen' hand luggage mysteriously turned up again, although I had to fill out countless forms to reclaim it. After just one night we were back off to Leningrad, where I managed to see two ballets, but the architecture struck me as over-decorative. And then it was back to the UK and the excitement of a new dishwasher.

But one last moment stuck in my mind for a long time: on the flight back from Leningrad, via Riga, I had a window seat. Shortly after take-off on the second leg, I was able to see Memel – or Klaipėda, as they call it now. I strained my eyes to see beyond, to the Haff, or beyond, to my former homeland of East Prussia… but in vain. That vision would have to wait for another day. I'd already waited over forty years, what difference would a few more make?

Lost for words

Few people have ever found me lost for words – although I may not always choose the right ones. But at around this time, in late 1990, many friends remarked on how I was 'not myself'. I would get halfway through a sentence, then… nothing. They would prompt me, gently suggest what I might have been meaning to say, but it was a total blank. And then the next sentence would again get to a midway stage, before…

Apparently my family thought it might have been due to the stress of looking after Tristan, whose health had deteriorated until in the middle of the year he died, peacefully in hospital. But my condition did not change afterwards: might I simply have been going senile? I always remember one lady in the village insisting that if she ever went 'gaga', we should tell her so. Of course, when it did happen, she was unable to take it in. In my case, however, I knew full well that something was missing, although what it might be was a mystery.

I had tests, and brain scans at the local hospital. None showed anything out of the ordinary, and all the doctors concluded it must indeed be the natural decay of old age. All except one. Shortly after Easter, Dr Meurig Williams called back the final image, paused a while, then pointed to one cloudy area saying, "I'm just wondering if that might be…". He called in a second opinion, and the expert consulted concurred that it was a tumour. Within just a few days, they had me in to Brook Hospital for surgery. As it was later explained to me – very much in layman's terms – they chopped open my skull, pulled it out together with a chunk of the brain, placed it on a table to slice out a piece around the size of a grapefruit, then stuck it back in again. And the results were remarkable.

People who visited before and after the operation said the transformation within just 24 hours was mind-blowing. My youngest son had returned from Japan with a partner, soon to be wife. When introduced, she had found me a quite docile person, evidently with no strong views to express, happy to go along with whatever others were saying. But when they visited the hospital just the day after the operation, she found me talking ten to the dozen, about anything and everything, as if making up for lost time – and highly opinionated too! Others said they were relieved I was back to 'normal', and pleased by the miraculous recovery modern medicine had brought about, but for her I think it was quite a shock. The shocks continued for a long time, and although I enjoyed her company immensely, it is my great regret that we never truly managed to get past the various cultural differences, such as our approaches to children, or attitudes to death – mine being one of the few biblical mottos I recalled: "Eat, drink, and be merry, for tomorrow we die!"

The route into the brain

Either way, I had now been given a new lease of life, and with no family commitments to hold me back, I felt myself brimming with energy to explore once again.

Africa!

First on the agenda was a trip south: below the Sahara. I had long been attracted by many facets of life in Africa. My eldest son had applied to do Voluntary Service Overseas, and been allocated to Sierra Leone… which he at first thought might be in South America, somewhat ironic considering that he went on to become a top academic in the field of African history! Before then, in 1957, my sister Marlene had been working at a school in Margate where the head suggested that she aim for something more exciting. On the spur of the moment she applied for a job in Tanzania, and got it. While there she met, and married, Peter, who was working in the cooperative movement. Mutti had visited them there in 1960, and commented on how familiar it felt, 'just like being back in East Prussia'. Peter's work later took them to many different countries, and in January 1992 they were in Nigeria, so I seized the opportunity to travel there, accompanied by my middle son Goronwy's Indian wife Rima.

It was just a week, in and around Kaduna, but the exotic environment was incredibly exciting – mango, papaya and cashew trees outside my window, bitter tomatoes whose leaves made a soup somewhat like sorrel, loofahs for loo-cleaning, calabashes used as floats by swimming fishermen, mushroom-shaped termite mounds, Jacaranda orchards, Dawadawa spices made from locust beans, colourful costumes, the unfamiliar rhythms of the Hausa language (which Marlene had somehow managed to pick up), glorious patterns on the Emir's Palace in Zaria, and lively, uninhibited children everywhere. Two years later I managed to go even further 'down', the first of two voyages to South Africa, and my children also helped arranged trips to Crete and Egypt in 1996, Canada 1999, then a cruise around the Baltic, all wonderful experiences which took me back to the travels of my youth.

Return to Mikalbude

Needless to say, however, at the forefront of my mind had always been some cherished hopes of revisiting my childhood home of Mikalbude. We enquired at various times during the Cold War, but the answer was always that any travel in that area was absolutely out of the question: the Iron Curtain was impenetrable.

Gradually however the tension between West and East began to thaw, and after Gorbachëv came to power and implemented his Glasnost / Perestroika programmes, my cousin Usch discovered that some resourceful West German travel agencies had begun to offer trips back to East Prussia – as they still referred to it.

In August 1992 therefore it came to be that Adam, his wife Mariko, his brother Goronwy and I all found ourselves leaving Usch's house in Hamburg to board a plane to Königsberg, now Kaliningrad. The tour was for ten days, during which time we stayed on the Baltic coast at a hotel in Svetlogorsk, or Rauschen as I still thought of it. Gisela's family had always spent their holidays at Rauschen because they loved the high coastline, with pine forests on top of the cliffs, whereas we had preferred the low, sandy beaches of Kranz.

We also met up with Irina, a keen Russian traveller who had suddenly befriended Marlene in a bookshop some years before. She had come there on the slow train from Moscow, where she and her daughter had a flat whose use she offered us. Some years later Adam and Mariko were there on the day the twin towers were attacked, and witnessed the shocked reactions of the Muscovites.

Over the next few days we had some organized excursions around the area, with one guide and two interpreters: Sandra, a friendly young student from Riga who was working at the hotel in Svetlogorsk, and Natasha, a Russian girl. When we went to visit the amber works at Palmnicken – an industrial complex far removed from my image of scavenging 'jewels' on the beach – Natasha went mad picking buckthorn on the dunes, bright orange berries which were deliciously sour but hard to get at because of the spikes. She later gave us some jam she had made from them.

Irina with sea buckthorn, delicious but spiky

While walking along the coast for a swim, we already found a café that had been started by an enterprising German refugee, complete with German waitresses. It was only serving German cakes though, no traditional East Prussian food. The hotel served mainly Russian food, as almost all guests, not to mention the staff, were Russian. The guests included several young children from the Chernobyl area, who had been sent for a short break by the sea. I recalled the Evans family in Birchington, who offered similar holidays each year to Chernobyl children, and who said that just one month in a healthy seaside environment apparently added a year to their lives.

Checking locations outside the Lada

130

It was interesting to look around the interior of Kaliningrad, which had changed dramatically since I last saw it some 45 years before. Our guide told us that 80% of the city had been destroyed in the last year of the war. However, our main interest was naturally to discover what had happened to Mikalbude.

Usch had sent us a map with the new Soviet names, from which we discovered that it was now called "Suchkovo". She had also told us of a taxi driver called Nikolai, who was employed by the hotel, and spoke good German as well as Russian, and we therefore engaged his services to take us there.

As we drew closer, I began to overlay the scenery on the map I had carried in my mind for so long. Suddenly I spotted the place where I used to catch the postbus to school in the morning. There was no sign of the hut that Väti had built to shelter me as I waited, but the location was unmistakeable. "There it is, up there on the hill – that's my home!" I cried.

Birch avenue

We drove slowly up the hill, along what used to be our birch avenue. When we reached the top, I felt rather bewildered. Instead of the familiar structures, there was a peculiar concrete water tower, presumably built by the Russians – none of the other buildings was intact. But soon I recognized the foundations of what used to be our own house, so we sat on our steps and had a picnic.

The steps, as now

The steps, a lifetime ago

As we wandered around afterwards, I managed to identify the stables – a single building housing a chicken coop, then a space for young foals, then the carriage horses, and finally the stables for the farm's workhorses. Even though the roof and upper parts had gone, the lower parts built of large fieldstones were still there, just as they had been. Next to this there was a place used for storing the horses' food, and adjoining that a shed for the dairy cows, where we could still see the chains to which the cows were tied, and their feeding troughs.

Stable ruins

Behind that we found our big pond, which we had used for skating. It had used to look so clean, but now was green and horrid. I remembered our cook lying there: she didn't go to swim, she just lay in the shallow end and let the leeches crawl all over her, which she seemed to enjoy. A sluice that was used to keep the water in, so the pond was always full but excess could be allowed to flow out into a ditch, had disappeared.

The other main farm building, at right angles, was our cow shed, which had contained 120 cattle as well as around 50 sheep. That was made of red brick, and most of the bricks were still there. The first part was a shed for the workers' cows, as each family had one or two cows for their own milk, and sometimes some sheep too, which I used to feed with pieces of swede.

There were no sheep here now. The fields too, had changed from being lush, verdant pasture full of juicy grass, to horrible steppe. In the distance we spotted a few meagre cows, guarded by a couple of men on horseback, so I resolved to ask them what had happened, using Nikolai as interpreter.

"Are there any people left who remember the farm how it was?"

"Some. Maybe."

The cowboys were not very forthcoming, indeed positively taciturn. Nikolai explained that they were wary in case we were trying to reclaim 'our' land. Apparently many other Germans had already come and voiced similar desires, even though the border had only been open for a short time. I tried to reassure them that we now lived in England and had no intention of trying to take back what had once been lost.

"There were soldiers first. Then their families came. They lived there."

He gestured to the workmen's houses.

"Now they live in Olëkhovo."

"Can you take us to see them?"

"Yes. We go now."

Checking Usch's map, I found that Olëkhovo was what used to be called Grieben, a small village just a few miles away. We climbed back into Nikolai's car, and followed the cowboys' horses down the birch avenue, then up the hill on the other side.

They brought us to a stop at a small house, with a goat tethered outside. A woman looking to be about the same age as me opened the door, and after a brief explanation by the cowboy invited the five of us in. Her name was Antonina.

Antonina and family

"I am from the Ukraine, but I was brought here when I was 18. I thought I was going to a factory nearby, but they made us come here to work like slaves."

134

She reminded me of Katya and Galya, who had both ended up on our farm via a similar route.

"My husband was a soldier. He came here with the army in 1945. I joined him in 1946, because Russia said we could all live together. He is dead now. His name was Muzhin."

My heart skipped a beat. Vitya's name had been Mosin. Could it be that they were related? But on this occasion the language barrier was too high.

She described how when they first arrived, nobody wanted to live in the big house, because they thought it would be much too cold. It was only some years later that a man came who was good at building the Russian kind of stove, where you could sleep on top. He built that in our – what used to be our – kitchen, so then some of the Ukrainians moved in there, rather than the smaller workmen's houses. They each grew their own vegetables and had their own fruit trees.

Later the new occupants moved to Olëkhovo, and people began to tear down the walls, because the bricks could be sold on the black market to Lithuanians, who took them to build houses in Lithuania. They sold many lorry loads. That explained why the lower walls, made of fieldstones, were still undisturbed.

At one moment, it struck me that Antonina's family had lived on 'our' farm longer than I had myself. How ridiculous then that Germans should now be returning to attempt to reclaim their property – would they insist that the thousands of Ukrainians, Belorussians and Russians were then repatriated to their parents' home towns and villages, to rediscover lives lost half a century before? The whole situation was unbearably tragic for all sides, but we had no choice other than to accept the status quo and try to build new friendships.

The Hall of Fame

135

Our time was limited, so having made friends with Antonina and promised to keep in contact, Nikolai took us back to the hotel. Most towns in the area seemed to have a Доска Почета (Hall of Fame) board, but many were dilapidated and empty. I took a photograph of their local one, and later filled it with her family's portraits as a Christmas card

In a car park near the hotel, Goronwy noticed a car with a conspicuous British numberplate.

"Well I never, she made it!" I thought. I was making an assumption, but it proved to be correct: I had told Virginia, a friend from St Nicholas-at-Wade, about our trip, and she had said she would try to join us en route, as she also had a friend in Nidden (now Nida), in Lithuania. We left a note under the windscreen wiper saying "We're in the café around the corner", and a little over an hour later she turned up, together with the Lithuanian friend.

Virginia described how she had driven through East Germany, Poland, Lithuania and Russia to get there, with numerous escapades involving visas, bribery and the like. She talked of them all in a very matter-of-fact way, but as she was the type to trek across Mongolia on horseback despite being only a little younger than me, her attitude did not surprise me. She was also a keen photographer, and had taken many beautiful images on her travels which made me realize that this was an aspect I had been ignoring, caught up in the present and the emotions of rediscovery. However, she also said she had had to be very cautious with any photography behind the Iron Curtain, to avoid being suspected of spying, and had consequently only taken a few generic shots of nature on this trip.

The following day we again had an optional, organized tour to Kranz, which was interesting if not so personally engaging. There was still one place I needed to visit, and we only had one free day left in which to do it. We had already booked Nikolai's services, and early the next morning he took us to Alischken – now called Karpovo – Omi's farm, which I had loved almost more than my own.

Alischken

How it stank now! Effluent was evidently flooding untreated into the Droje – the river[19] – and it smelt like a sewer. The wonderful house at Alischken had vanished, just as at Mikalbude, but the rest was in better shape – the stable and the bell tower granary were both very much intact. Mariko climbed up to the first floor above the stable, where hay had been kept, and waved to us out of the window. But it was plainly deserted, with nobody around to ask about what had happened in the intervening period. There were just vast fields of sunflowers, probably being farmed for their oil. Despite the stench, it was still a beautiful place.

We wandered down through Omi's park to the Droje, and Goronwy – ever the adventurer – found a tree that had fallen in, so climbed across at the place we had called the *pakrausch*. My heart was in my mouth, as I knew that although the park side was quite shallow, the river was much deeper on the far side, with fast currents.

---

[19] As with human settlements, natural features have also all been renamed: the *Droje* is now the *Гремячья* = *Gremyach'ya*

I had once nearly lost two horses there, and had sworn never again to challenge the Droje. Still, he made it across, and then adamantly refused to come back, because the park side was full of stinging nettles, and mosquitos too. It really was in a terrible condition.

Alischken

We continued walking along opposite banks, until we reached a road bridge. I wondered if this had replaced the little footbridge where we used to play Pooh-sticks, and where Onkel Arnold had fished for crayfish, by sliding his hands under the stones on the park side.

Fishing in the *Droje*

137

There we found a fisherman, Sergei, angling just as we had when young. He said the water was getting bad, and the fish were not good. From his age, I guessed that he'd been there since 1946, but he made no comment about what had become of the farm itself. We exchanged addresses, though, and said we would write. Neither he nor Antonina had a telephone – even the hotel only had one for shared use, as with the bathroom and television set.

Suchkovo revisited

Less than a year after our first trip, Adam and Mariko again accompanied me to Kaliningradskaya Oblast – already I did not think of it as East Prussia. This time we were accompanied not by another son, but by my cousins Heidi, Usch and Kurt-Ulrich. One of my aims was to take more photographs, particularly of Alischken, to supplement those taken on the first trip. I had been writing to Antonina in the meantime, as well as to the fisherman, and we managed to visit both of them again, once more driven by Nikolai in his ancient Lada – which proved more reliable than a Western Volvo his rival Yevgeny was proudly exhibiting.

Trinkt Kathreiner!
A coffee advertisement, not an important military sign as its new owner had thought

But where, oh where, was Alischken? The paradise of my childhood… it was hard even to find the paths we had travelled just one year before. The ramshackle bridge had decayed further, and the roofs collapsed. At Mikalbude too, we saw piles of bricks showing that people were plundering the site for whatever materials they could – allegedly, they were of such quality that it was worth coming from Lithuania to sell them there. Gradually, it was going to revert to a peat bog, to lush countryside populated by deer, storks and elk, with only a few stones to bear witness to people who had once called it home. And that was what I truly hoped – that would make it paradise once more.

Alischken, just a year later

Nature reclaims the granary

Human history begins to fade

Antonina and her family had their own homes, warm homes – maybe no indoor lavatory, but complete with banya, steam rooms like saunas where they gently beat us with birch twigs… or not so gently in Adam's case. And they were already into four generations, and they seemed happy there. Who could not be?

With Ira, Antonina's grand-daughter

Only Usch still seemed to bear some resentment. Her family had fought tooth and nail after the end of the war to try and reclaim their land, continuing writing to international bodies even in the 1990s, arguing about the terms of the Hague and Geneva Conventions. But eventually – or perhaps so far – all in vain.

Via the *Angerapper Heimatbrief*, a periodical for people who used to live in that area, I had also resumed contact with Hanna, a schoolfriend I had not seen since that time, and she described her own visit back in a letter to me:

Dear Anneli,

I got back from northern East Prussia a few days ago. It was a sad, but also beautiful trip. The journey with the coach was pleasant, and on the way there, we spent a night at Thorn, where I met a couple of dear friends. The stop at Deutsch-Eylau took only two hours, then they waved us on without checking. In Königsberg we switched to a Russian coach, which brought us via Wehlau, Norkitten and Insterburg to Gumbinnen. We slept at the homes of Russian families, who lent us their apartments and spent that time with friends or relatives. There is a public bar in the town, and that's where we had our meals – the food was very good. The coach drove us around the area every day.

We spent two days at Skirlack... which of course doesn't exist anymore. We drove from Angerapp, via Kowarren, past Mikalbude to Skirlack. The coach stopped at the ruins of Kröhn's Inn, and we (there were 38 of us) searched for our houses. Scrambling over fields and ditches, each one managed to find his or her former home. Many bushes, old trees, overgrown ponds, springs and foundations are still present, yet the landscape has altered completely, as all the paths and buildings are gone. It was fantastic to meet my fellow travellers again. The mood was good once we got beyond the first depressing day, and we enjoyed the evenings at the local bar. But I was so disappointed by Angerapp, Trempen, Insterburg and Königsberg, I could have wept. The poverty of the countryside is unbearable. Yet above all we were blessed with a wonderful summer sky, and a huge number of storks' nests. I have enclosed here a picture of them: the true inhabitants of Skirlack.

Your Hanna

In May 1995, Marlene and Peter took me to visit Jutta in Magdeburg, but en route we visited Frieda, the maid from Mikalbude whom I had not seen since. Mutti had kept in touch with her Mamma[20], Frau Schalonka, ever since our flight from East Prussia. They had ended up in Mecklenburg, the northern part of East Germany, and Frieda still lived there, with her son Dieter and his family. Dieter was actually my one and only god-son – much good that did him! He had been baptized before we left Mikalbude, although I can't remember if it was at our church in Trempen or by a fleeting visit of the pastor to our farm.

As part of *Lastenausgleich*, Frau Schalonka's family had been given a small farm, just as Claus had. But she used to complain constantly to Mutti that although she

---

[20] Henriette Schalonka was actually Frieda's aunt, but primarily responsible for her upbringing; her mother, Auguste Butsadotski, she called Mutti.

had been a proper farmer's wife and always cherished the thought of having her own homestead, in reality she found it to be too much responsibility, and was dismayed at how much produce they had to supply in lieu of taxes.

Mutti had not been permitted to attend her funeral, but had stayed in touch with Frieda, although never met up. I was glad of the opportunity, so we headed off along the Baltic coast, staying in guesthouses near picturesque lakes where we could hear frogs croaking all night, and nightingales singing in the garden, as identified by Peter. One of these was the Cambsersee, close to Schwerin and the village where she lived. Marlene had Frieda's address and was confident she could find the house… but after two hours, asking locals and being sent pillar to post, we arrived to find that Dieter had already had to leave. His wife came back briefly to say hello with their son, who appears to have quite a severe mental disability, and stayed to share some red Krimsekt, our traditional celebratory drink. Frieda needed crutches to walk, but otherwise seemed quite comfortable – her farm cottage was far more comfortable than even the main house at Mikalbude had been, with running water and a proper bathroom, even a garage in place of the former cow shed.

Frieda and family

After visiting some more lakes, we went on to Berlin, hoping to find Lori Schneider, the daughter of Mutti's friend from finishing school, who had come to Mikalbude every summer and also visited me in Vienna. But again, despite having an address we failed to find her. We also experienced problems keeping in touch with Frieda later – just having an address was no guarantee that letters would arrive, and both sides tended to think the other was ignoring them. The arrival of new forms of communication such as e-mail does not seem to have improved this situation much.

Across the border

In 2002, Adam decided we could visit some other locations from my childhood on the other side of the border: in other words, the part of East Prussia that had been 'claimed' by Poland. Thus in August, shortly after Street Acre visits by Irina and Hanna, I made my third trip down memory lane, to the Masurian lakes. We drove from his house near Leipzig, passing fields full of windmills which looked to me like gymnasts or break dancers, and some fascinating basketwork sculptures at the Polish border symbolizing dialogue between the two nations. Once in Poland our dialogue was more stilted, having to rely on single words in a dictionary, but we still managed to find a motel with a hot bath – and good bathplugs, which I had missed on our second return journey to East Prussia – and a restaurant serving soup inside large crusty loaves of sourdough bread.

Parts of our journey suffered detours due to extensive floods, but after some interesting cultural diversions en route – excellent open-air museums and the like – we eventually arrived at Wuttrienen (now Butryny), where I had been compelled to perform Labour Service some sixty years before. I had not been able to find it on any map, but Adam had identified it and taken me there as a surprise. Yet nothing looked familiar by now, except the storks on their high nests, and the beautiful sunset over the lake. We pressed on further north, and came to the Wolfsschanze, Hitler's huge complex of bunkers, where the ill-fated assassination plot by Adam's namesake had taken place. It felt gruesome, and I thought back to Feliks Zarod, the Jewish lawyer my mother had foolishly requested be sent back to his family in Warsaw. Leaving that behind, we next visited the von Fahrenheid pyramid – a bizarre mausoleum to the family who had owned the land on which my father and grandfather had been tenant farmers. The coffins were still inside, but lay empty, like their farmsteads.

Finally, we reached Żabin, or as I remembered it, Szabienen. It was about 14 km from Mikalbude, as the crow flies, which now would be the best way to travel between the two, as the distance by road would have been twice as long, and involve all the palaver of crossing the Russian border. This was where my father's father, Opa, had lived, but when we asked after his farm, we were shown a comparatively new building standing on the site with no trace of what I remembered. However, the next day we managed have a perfect day, swimming in Jezioro Święcajty, a beautiful lake where in summer I used to boat, and in winter watch sail races on the ice. We spent the rest of the day looking at folk art and enjoying yeast cake, just as my grandmother had used to bake here when the country had a different name. All that was lacking was the excitement of some wild boars, although they were reputed to be in the area.

The true inhabitants resume residence

Loose Ends

As with the earlier volume *Reflections in an Oval Mirror*, these memoirs mention hundreds of people, ranging from young children and family friends up to the most famous personages of the day. In an ideal world we would include an index, together with significant biographical details where known. That task would however take another decade, so here we have simply included outlines of those who played a major part in Anneli's life or the events told in her books, for those curious to know 'what happened later?'.

East Prussian connections

Lucien Lebrun died in 1993, as a result of a car crash just 50 m from his son's home; they had been en route to celebrate his other son's birthday.

Feliks Zarod, the Jewish lawyer Anneli had been so concerned about, survived the war and went on to work in Polish politics until his death in 1987.

Little Volodya remarried shortly before emigrating to Australia, but they soon separated and he moved to Sydney with his father, Mark, and married a third time before dying there in 1988.

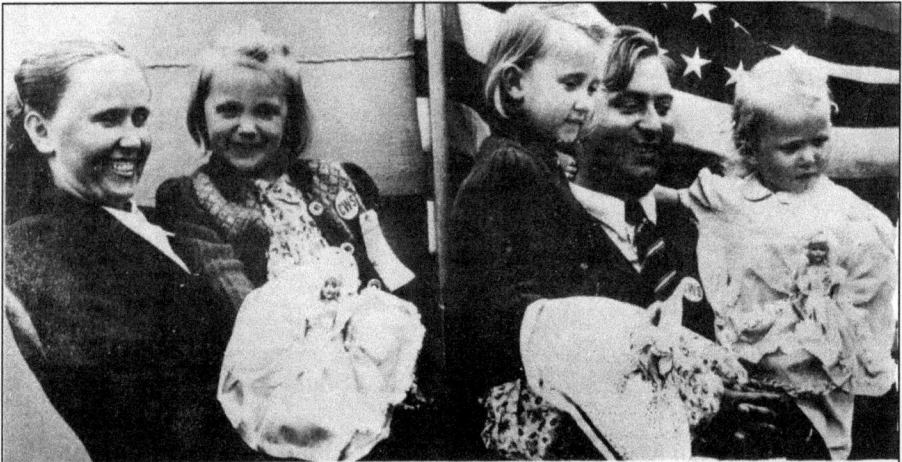

Religious News Service Photo

Volodymyr Holubiw, the 250,000th DP admitted to the United States, disembarking with his family. He was sponsored by the Assemblies of God.

250,000th Displaced Person
Sponsored by Assemblies

Big Volodya and Marusha achieved their fifteen minutes of fame when entering the US, and went on to become very successful farmers in Wisconsin. Their sponsor virtually adopted them, they in turn treated him like a father, and ended up owning his farm. Volodya and Marusha had two more children, several grandchildren, and died in 1989 and 2014 respectively.

Karl-Heinz Caspari continued to be a prominent writer and director, particularly in television; he died in 2009.

News Guardian and Observer connections

'Bill' from the News Guardian continued in journalism for a time, then became chief PR officer for the UK Atomic Energy Authority. He died in 1996, a few years before his daughter – through pure chance – ended up moving near St Nicholas-at-Wade and becoming friends with one of Anneli's sons.

'Cliff' joined the BBC, rapidly rose through the ranks, revolutionized TV news at ITN, and continued at Anglia and Tyne-Tees, earning an OBE. He died in 2010.

Del Flatley covered the Nuremberg trials, and later became president of the Institute of Journalists and a member of the Press Council, earning an MBE. He died in 1992.

Charles Reid went on to be music critic of the Spectator, and write well-received biographies of Barbirolli, Beecham and Sargent.

Ken Obank and dozens of other former Observer staff, including Anneli, Bob Stephens, Chris Bielenberg and more, used to attend regular FOBS (Friends of the OBServer) meetings organized by Gritta Weill until numbers dwindled through old age and death. David Astor himself was one of Tristan's best friends, and remained close to Anneli too until his death in 2001.

David and Anneli in 2000 at the memorial for Eirene

Taqui continued to visit Anneli from her home in Dorking, until a few years before her death in 2001. There are countless accounts of the story behind *Swallows and Amazons*, but her own memoirs were published as *In Aleppo Once* and *Chimes from a Wooden Bell*. Her brother, Roger Altounyan, used his experience as an airman to invent the Intal 'spin inhaler' treatment for asthma, and died quite young, partly due to his experimentation on himself – brilliantly portrayed by David Suchet in the film *Hair Soup*. Taqui's son 'Chimpy' (Roger) became a post-punk playwright, and wrote a book called Minnows (see page 99), while his brother Nicky became a renowned woodworker and art teacher; he died in 2020.

Gisèle Aton remained in Avignon, working in the arts. After many years of assuming Anneli was dead (and vice versa), they resumed regular correspondence in 2004. She died in 2016.

Others

Arthur Lall had a stellar career, becoming India's ambassador to the United Nations. The marriage with Susheila failed – she divorced him, suffered from substance abuse and was murdered by her servants; their daughter Tookie died in her 30s.

Khushwant Singh similarly became a household name, primarily as a very witty writer; he died in 2014. His daughter Mala (Dayal) continues to work as a writer and editor.

Family

Mutti gradually grew frailer, and for the last period of her life moved to be with Marlene in Leicestershire. Although she could still look out over a 'proper garden', in other words one full of produce to eat, rather than purely decorative, she was largely confined to bed – her 'deathbed' as she called it – and frequently commented that "they treat dogs better", meaning that animals could be euthanized once they were past their 'useful' life. She eventually found her peace in 1986, and her ashes were scattered in the Baltic in the hope that at least some of them would end up again in East Prussia.

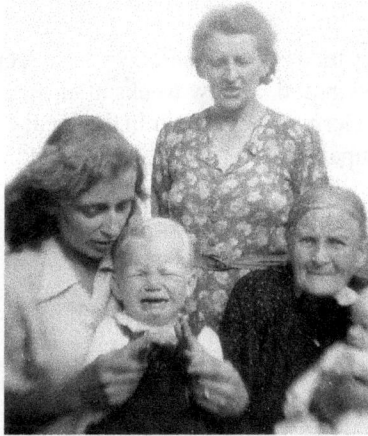

Four camera-shy generations

Tristan retired from the Observer and devoted himself to collecting coaches, commemorative ceramics and other antiques. He died in 1990; his funeral, typically eccentric, was widely covered in the local press, and the sale of his collection attracted national attention. His sister Eirene became a life peer, and died just before the turn of the millennium.

Tristan
waves
goodbye

Tristan says goodbye.   TT1193/24

FORMER journalist Tristan Jones waved goodbye to his colourful life on Friday.

As his chipboard coffin was wheeled into St. Nicholas Church on Friday, a waving hand — of the type usually seen in the back of Ford Escorts — bade a fond farewell to the mourners.

From their home "Street Acre", his widow Annelie said:

"The funeral was Tristan's idea, he knew how he wanted to go and had it planned for years.

"The coffin was made of chipboard because it was

To back page

Tristan's sons draw his chipboard coffin to church as other family members watch.
TT1193/15

TRISTAN
WAVES
GOODBYE

From page 1

cheap and the hand was his way of saying a final good-bye."

The cortege was led by his pet dog Rhodri.

Tristan, who died at the age of 77, was the general manager of The Observer and an important influence on its post-war history.

He was one of Fleet Street's most colourful and engaging characters.

He joined the paper in the late 1940s as a Saturday sub-editor, worked for several years on the foreign news service and became general manager in 1953.

Wishing to avoid emotional farewells, he left the Observer in 1975 without telling the staff or even his chauffeur, who drove to collect him as usual.

Tristan leaves a widow, Annelie, three sons and two daughters.

Tristan's funeral

Claus gave up farming to work in insurance, near Verden, but kept breeding Trakehner horses. He died in 2003, a few weeks after the siblings' last meeting.

Jutta remained in East Germany, involved in the local church, and died in 2019.

Marlene continued campaigning for peace, even spending time in jail in her late sixties. She died in 2019 – her own memoirs are published as *Skating at the Edge of the Wood*.

As for Anneli herself, she continued to be a 'revolting granny', protesting against the Iraq War and attending (and loving) her first punk concert at the age of 81. She died on 29 October 2011, in hospital after a routine operation. Her funeral was full of flowers, featured music from her children, and was described by an old friend who attended as "just like a wonderful wedding". Her burial was an ecological one, in the village cemetery next door to Street Acre – but in her party dress.

ANNELI JONES
Née Anneliese Wiemer
Born 8th May 1923
In Mikalbude, East Prussia
Lived at Street Acre
For 61 Years
Died 29th October 2011

At peace

Tu ne quaesieris, scire nefas, quem mihi, quem tibi
finem di dederint, Leuconoe, nec Babylonios
temptaris numeros. ut melius, quidquid erit, pati.
seu pluris hiemes seu tribuit Iuppiter ultimam,
quae nunc oppositis debilitat pumicibus mare
Tyrrhenum. Sapias, vina liques et spatio brevi
spem longam reseces. dum loquimur, fugerit invida
aetas: carpe diem, quam minimum credula postero.

Ask not ('tis forbidden knowledge), what our destined term of years,
Mine and yours; nor scan the tables of your Babylonish seers.
Better far to bear the future, my Leuconoe, like the past,
Whether Jove has many winters yet to give, or this our last;
This, that makes the Tyrrhene billows spend their strength against the shore.
Strain your wine and prove your wisdom; life is short; should hope be more?
In the moment of our talking, envious time has ebb'd away.
Seize the present; trust tomorrow e'en as little as you may.

Quintus Horatius Flaccus, Carmina, Liber I, Carmen XI
translated by John Conington

149

Herr: es ist Zeit. Der Sommer war sehr groß
Leg deinen Schatten auf die Sonnenuhren,
und auf den Fluren laß die Winde los.
Befiehl den letzten Früchten voll zu sein;
gieb ihnen noch zwei südlichere Tage,
dränge sie zur Vollendung hin und jage
die letzte Süße in den schweren Wein.
Wer jetzt kein Haus hat, baut sich keines mehr.
Wer jetzt allein ist, wird es lange bleiben,
wird wachen, lesen, lange Briefe schreiben
und wird in den Alleen hin und her
unruhig wandern, wenn die Blätter treiben.

Lord: the hour is upon us. It was a good summer.
Lay now thy shadow upon the sundials,
Let the winds roam the fields freely,
Leave not the last fruits half-full,
Give unto them two more days of sun,
Lead them to perfection, deliver the last drops
Of sweetness to our strong wine.
She who has no home now will build none for herself.
She who is alone now will long remain so,
Will watch, read, write long letters
And wander eagerly to and fro
Driven as a leaf before the wind.

Rilke (Herbsttag)

Chronology

8 May 1945	Anneli's 22nd birthday; war in Europe ends, she starts working for Military Government, and meets Tristan
August 1945	Mikalbude/Mickelau renamed Suchkovo, within Soviet Union
Spring 1946	Works for News Guardian
October 1947	Works for The Observer and Stephens in Berlin
July 1948	With TJ in Aberystwyth, and Stephens in Coniston and Barnes
December 1949	Family life with Tristan begins
October 1950	First child (of five) born
October 1955	TJ dies
May 1982	Lebrun visits
November 1986	Mutti dies
8 May 1988	First visitors from East Germany
April 1989	Trip to Siberia
June 1990	Tristan dies
January 1991	First grandchild (of five) born
April 1991	First brain tumour operated
Jan 1992	Trip to Nigeria
August 1992	First trip back to Mikalbude
July 1993	Second trip back to Mikalbude
Jan 1994	Trip to South Africa
March 1998	Second brain tumour operated
August 2002	Third trip back to East Prussia, from Polish side (Masuria)
October 2003	Claus dies
8 May 2008	*Reflections in an Oval Mirror* published
29 October 2011	Anneli dies
December 2019	Marlene dies
29 October 2021	*Reflections* published in German translation
8 May 2023	*Carpe Diem* published

Mikalbude maps

More detailed maps, along with various links and suggestions for further reading, can be found via https://ozaru.net/ozarubooks/eastprussia.html

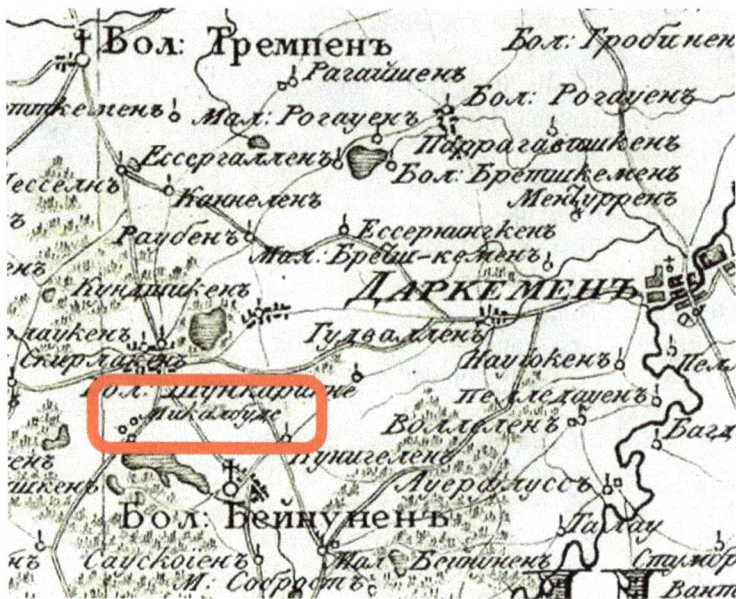

Mikalbude on a Russian map, 1820

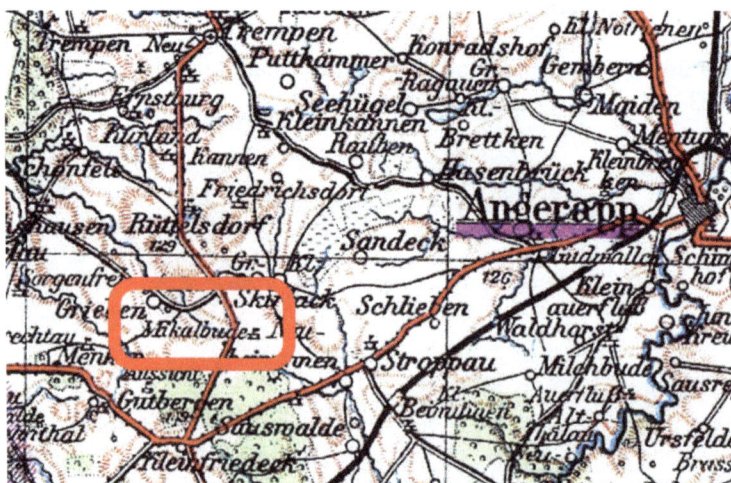

Mikalbude on a German map, 1919

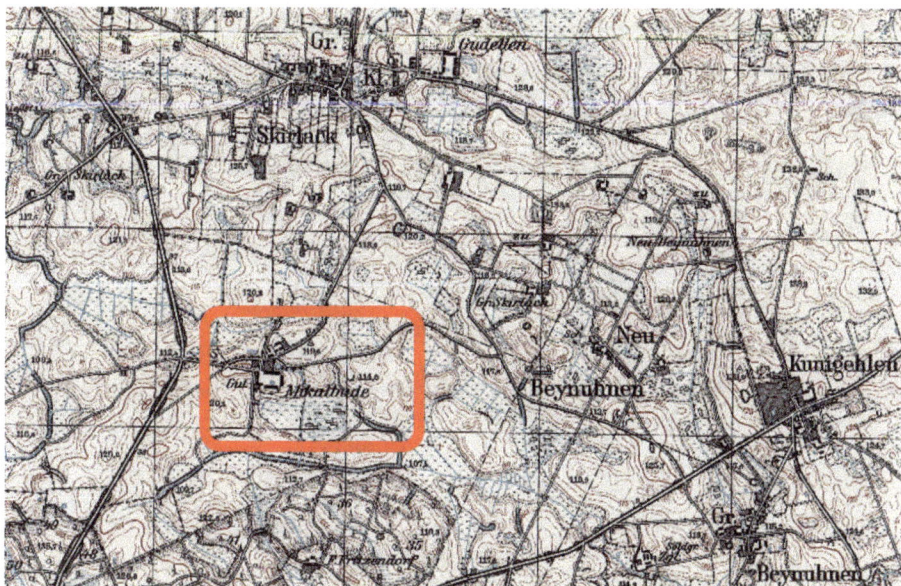
Gut Mikalbude on a German map, 1927

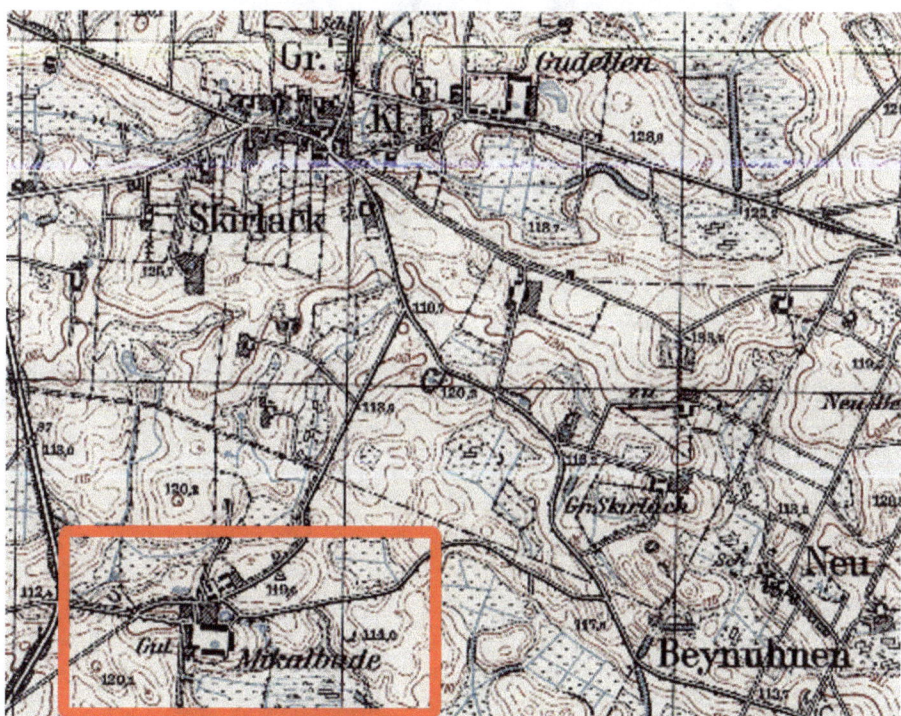
Gut Mikalbude on a German map, 1936

Mickelau on a German map, 1941

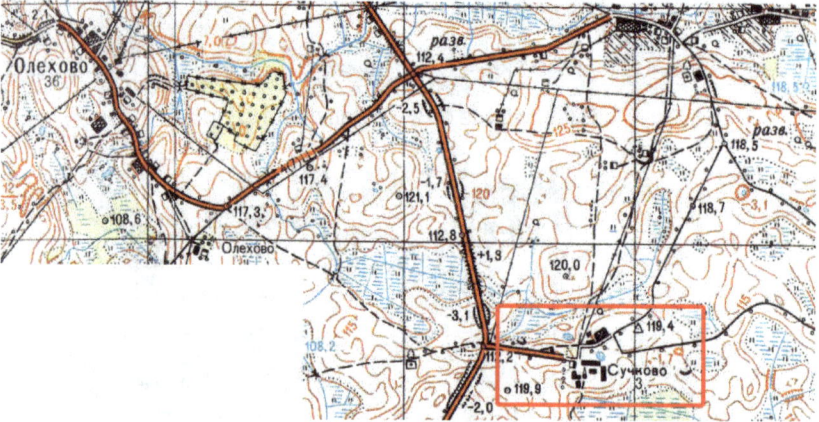

Suchkovo on a Russian map, 1955; Olëkhovo is to the left

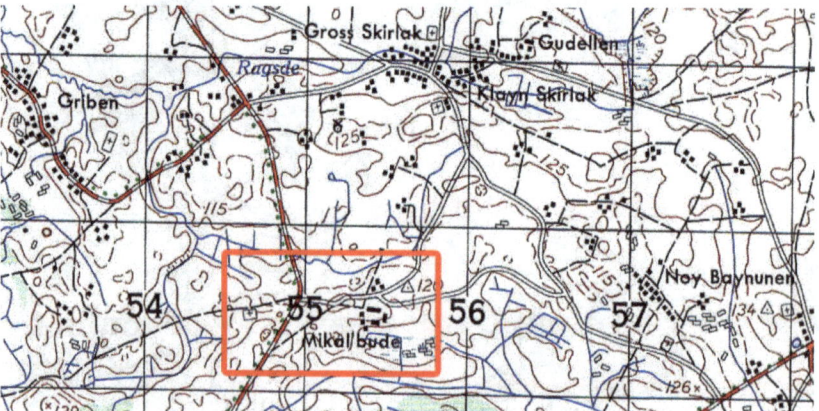

Mikalbude on an American map, 1958; note the old names

154

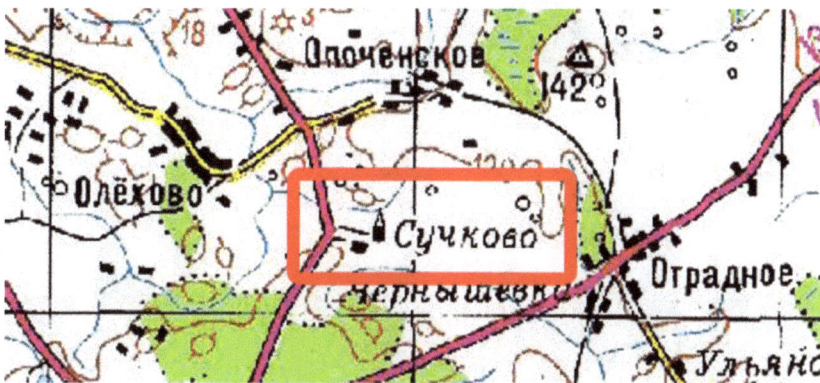
Suchkovo on a Russian military map, 1985

Suchkovo on a Russian map, 1986

Suchkovo on a Russian map, 2000

155

Russian map, 2001; only Olëkhovo is named

Russian map, 2007

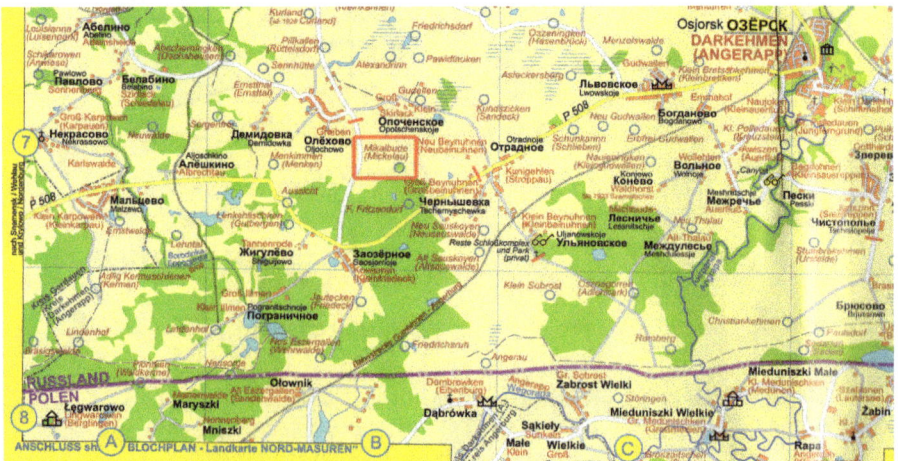
Full circle: Mikalbude (Mickelau) but no Suchkovo, on a 2020 map from www.blochplan.de
© BLOCHPLAN, Berlin

Other publications from Ōzaru Books

Ōzaru Books is a boutique publisher based in the Thanet village of St Nicholas-at-Wade. Our primary focus is on books with a local connection, ranging from creative writing by East Kent authors to (occasionally niche) scholarly tomes about Kentish history, but we have a secondary interest in works in translation, particularly from Eastern languages, and also tales from East Prussia. Some of our profits go to support gorilla charities, which is the origin of the name Ōzaru ('Great Ape') and our logo.

Reflections in an Oval Mirror
Memories of East Prussia, 1923–45
Anneli Jones

8 May 1945 – VE Day – was Anneliese Wiemer's twenty-second birthday. Although she did not know it then, it marked the end of her flight to the West, and the start of a new life in England.

These illustrated memoirs, based on a diary kept during the Third Reich and letters rediscovered many decades later, depict the momentous changes occurring in Europe against a backcloth of everyday farm life in East Prussia (now the north-western corner of Russia, sandwiched between Lithuania and Poland).

The political developments of the 1930s (including the Hitler Youth, 'Kristallnacht', political education, labour service, war service, and interrogation) are all the more poignant for being told from the viewpoint of a romantic young girl. In lighter moments she also describes student life in Vienna and Prague, and her friendship with Belgian and Soviet prisoners of war. Finally, however, the approach of the Red Army forces her to abandon her home and flee across the frozen countryside, encountering en route a cross-section of society ranging from a 'lady of the manor', worried about her family silver, to some concentration camp inmates

"couldn't put it down...delightful...very detailed descriptions of the farm and the arrival of war...interesting history and personal account" ('Rosie', amazon.co.uk)

"Anneli did not fully conform but she still survived, and how this happened is the real gem...There is optimism, humour, great affection and a tremendous sense of adventure in a period when this society was hurtling towards disaster." ('Singapore Relic', amazon.co.uk)

ISBN: 978-0-9559219-0-2

Also available on Kindle

German translation (with colourized photographs) available as ISBN 978-1-915174-00-0

Skating at the Edge of the Wood
Memories of East Prussia, 1931–1945...1993
Marlene Yeo

In 1944, the twelve-year old East Prussian girl Marlene Wiemer embarked on a horrific trek to the West, to escape the advancing Red Army. Her cousin Jutta was left behind the Iron Curtain, which severed the family bonds that had made the two so close.

This book contains dramatic depictions of Marlene's flight, recreated from her letters to Jutta during the last year of the war, and contrasted with joyful memories of the innocence that preceded them.

Nearly fifty years later, the advent of perestroika meant that Marlene and Jutta were finally able to revisit their childhood home, after a lifetime of growing up under diametrically opposed societies, and the book closes with a final chapter revealing what they find.

Despite depicting the same time and circumstances as "Reflections in an Oval Mirror", an account written by Marlene's elder sister, Anneli, and its sequel "Carpe Diem", this work stands in stark contrast partly owing to the age gap between the two girls, but above all because of their dramatically different characters.

"Marlene Yeo's account of living on a well to do farm is very engaging and her description of some of the small details of picking mushrooms in the woods, baking rye bread and skating in winter all brought the great political tragedy of the region down to an understandably human level for the non German reader ... the description of desolation at the end of the book was heart breaking. " (Jonathon M Stenner, amazon.co.uk)

"Fantastic autobiography – beautifully written! Gives real insight into life and times in rural East Prussia in 1930s and 1940s. One of the best of several autobiographies of this period that I have read." (Mrs C.J. Pedley, amazon.co.uk)

" Fascinating look at a brutally ethnically cleansed province ... This book was so interesting, I read it very quickly ... The author does a great job of describing farm life in East Prussia as well as the chaos and insanity in that province in the waning days of the war. Gripping and highly recommended." (R. Miller, amazon.com)

ISBN: 978-0-9931587-2-8

Also available on Kindle

German translation (with colourized photographs) available as ISBN 978-1-915174-01-7

Animal Guising and the Kentish Hooden Horse

James Frost

Published to accompany a four-month exhibition at Maidstone Museum, this book builds on Maylam's "The Hooden Horse" and Frampton's "Discordant Comicals" to expand the field of study into East Kent's unique folk custom: what hoodening was, what the hooden horse is, and how it can be seen in the national context of animal guising. It covers historical records and artifacts, revival groups, "Autohoodening" performances which reimagine the old tradition in a modern context, and related practices such as the Mari Lwyd, Obby Osses, various northern beasts, and stag guising. Appendices contain the text of numerous contemporary verses and plays.

The author, James Frost, is a Lecturer in Performing Arts at Canterbury Christ Church University, as well as a Senior Fellow of the Higher Education Academy. He has also made numerous hooden horses and similar beasts, and performed with the Canterbury Hoodeners.

The book features over 60 full colour illustrations, many never seen before in print.

"[an] essential purchase [...] generously and informatively illustrated [...] a fascinating volume that at once informs, intrigues and entertains" (Tykes' Stirrings)

"stands alone as a scholarly re-examination of the Kentish ritual ... a detailed account ... beautifully and extensively illustrated ... right up to date ... fascinating and absorbing ... a comprehensive bibliography and an extensive appendix [with] a beautifully evocative first-hand account of what it is like to be a hoodener" (Folk London)

ISBN: 978-1-915174-06-2

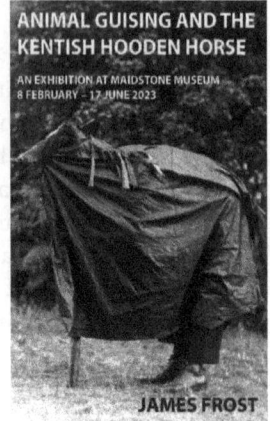

Discordant Comicals – The Hooden Horse of East Kent
George Frampton

Hoodening is an ancient calendar custom unique to East Kent, involving a wooden horse's head on a pole, carried by a man concealed by a sack. The earliest reliable record is from 1735, but other than Percy Maylam's seminal work "The Hooden Horse", published in 1909 (republished in an annotated edition in 2021: see below), little serious research has gone into the tradition.

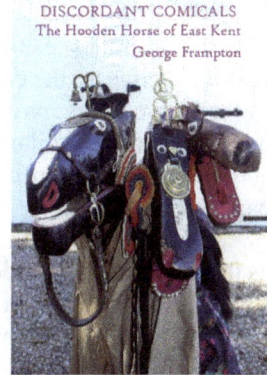

DISCORDANT COMICALS
The Hooden Horse of East Kent
George Frampton

George Frampton has rectified this, by cross-referencing dozens of newspaper reports, census records and other accounts to build a comprehensive picture of who the Hoodeners were, why (and where) they did it, and how it related to other folk traditions.

He then goes beyond Maylam to look at the 'demise' of Hoodening in around 1921, its widely heralded 'revival' in 1966, and discovers that this narrative is in fact quite misleading, as several Hooden Horses were still active throughout that period. He includes descriptions of the current teams, and supplies plentiful appendices detailing past participants, places visited, songs performed, events on Hoodening's timeline, and the horses themselves.

Full indices make it easy for modern Men and Maids of Kent to check whether their ancestors might have been involved, and detailed references make this an invaluable resource for social historians too.

The book features over 70 full colour illustrations.

"a good read for the interested layman as well as a valuable resource for anyone interested in the custom" (The Morris Dancer)

"very readable research [...] backed up with generous quotations [...] reveals a tale of rich cultural heritage." (The Living Tradition)

"thoroughly researched [...] well presented [...] full of previously un-published interviews [...] in depth analysis [...] extremely interesting" (Around Kent Folk)

"provides a sense of the scope and history of the rarely studied practice of hoodening [...] offers the most up-to-date and comprehensive starting point for any scholar interested in the practice" (The Journal of Folklore Research)

"attractively published in hardback with numerous colour illustrations [...] A lot of admirable spadework and academic endeavour [...] copious references are given throughout" (Master Mummers)

"Frampton has left no stone unturned in his research [...] there is a very useful index, which helps make this a book to dip into profitably" (Archæologia Cantiana)

"profusely illustrated and printed in colour, it's a treat for the eyes [...] meticulous and detailed [...] a compelling and intriguing volume" (Tykes' News)

ISBN: 978-0-9559219-7-3

The Hooden Horse of East Kent – Annotated Edition
Percy Maylam

Percy Maylam's "The Hooden Horse: an East Kent Christmas Custom" was long the definitive work on Hoodening – indeed, the only full-scale study of the custom. It covered the current practice in Thanet at the start of the 20th century, past printed records, theories about its possible demise, similar customs in other parts of England and Germany, and speculation about its ancient, possibly pagan origins.

Although Frampton has arguably superseded Maylam as the authority on Hoodeners and their activities, his book still takes Maylam as a basis to explore what happened since his time. Maylam's original work is indispensable even now, but the first format is very rare, as only 303 copies were printed, and only a reduced edition appeared later.

This new eBook includes the whole of Maylam's text, with numerous features to help those wanting to push the research further – even those lucky enough to have a copy of the 1909 hardback. There are copious annotations, internal hyperlinks, images of and external links to original sources, and appendices with contemporary reviews. The eBook naturally allows readers to search the whole text, yet the page numbers are still present to enable cross-referencing to Frampton and others (N.B. some of the functionality may vary, depending on the device used to read the book). The list of subscribers (which was omitted from another edition) is present, along with brief biographical notes on many of them, to show who was reading Maylam and what impact he would have had at the time.

The book is therefore a vital source of information for anyone interested in folk drama, including mumming. It is rigorously academic by the standards of the day, but also remains readable for general fans of the genre. This edition also contains updated versions of the early 20C photographs.

Available on Kindle

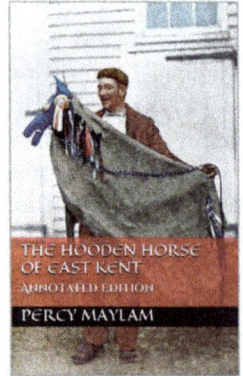

The Margate Tales
Stephen Channing

Chaucer's Canterbury Tales is without doubt one of the best ways of getting a feel for what the people of England in the Middle Ages were like. In the modern world, one might instead try to learn how different people behave and think from television or the internet.

However, to get a feel for what it was like to be in Margate as it gradually changed from a small fishing village into one of Britain's most popular holiday resorts, one needs to investigate contemporary sources such as newspaper reports and journals.

Stephen Channing has saved us this work, by trawling through thousands of such documents to select the most illuminating and entertaining accounts of Thanet in the 18th and early to mid 19th centuries. With content ranging from furious battles in the letters pages, to hilarious pastiches, witty poems and astonishing factual reports, illustrated with over 70 drawings from the time, The Margate Tales brings the society of the time to life, and as with Chaucer, demonstrates how in many areas, surprisingly little has changed.

"substantial and fascinating volume…meticulously researched…an absorbing read"
(Margate Civic Society)

ISBN: 978-0-9559219-5-7

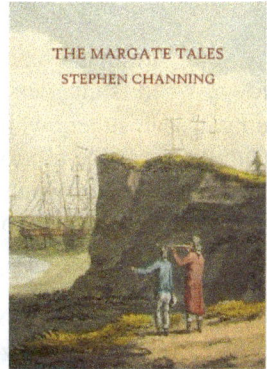

Turner's Margate Through Contemporary Eyes
– The Viney Letters –
Stephen Channing

Margate in the early 19th century was an exciting town, where smugglers and 'preventive men' fought to outwit each other, while artists such as JMW Turner came to paint the glorious sunsets over the sea. One of the young men growing up in this environment decided to set out for Australia to make his fortune in the Bendigo gold rush.

Half a century later, having become a pillar of the community, he began writing a series of letters and articles for Keble's Gazette, a publication based in his home town. In these, he described Margate with great familiarity (and tremendous powers of recall), while at the same time introducing his English readers to the "latitudinarian democracy" of a new, "young Britain".

Viney's interests covered a huge range of topics, from Thanet folk customs such as Hoodening, through diatribes on the perils of assigning intelligence to dogs, to geological theories including suggestions for the removal of sandbanks off the English coast "in obedience to the sovereign will and intelligence of man".

His writing is clearly that of a well-educated man, albeit with certain Victorian prejudices about the colonies that may make those with modern sensibilities wince a little. Yet above all, it is interesting because of the light it throws on life in a British seaside town some 180 years ago.

This book also contains numerous contemporary illustrations.

"profusely illustrated...draws together a series of interesting articles and letters...recommended" (Margate Civic Society)

ISBN: 978-0-9559219-2-6

A Victorian Cyclist
– Rambling through Kent in 1886 –
Stephen & Shirley Channing

Bicycles are so much a part of everyday life nowadays, it can be surprising to realize that for the late Victorians these "velocipedes" were a novelty disparaged as being unhealthy and unsafe – and that indeed tricycles were for a time seen as the format more likely to succeed.

Some people however adopted the new-fangled devices with alacrity, embarking on adventurous tours throughout the countryside. One of them documented his 'rambles' around East Kent in such detail that it is still possible to follow his routes on modern cycles, and compare the fauna and flora (and pubs!) with those he vividly described.

In addition to providing today's cyclists with new historical routes to explore, and both naturalists and social historians with plenty of material for research, this fascinating book contains a special chapter on Lady Cyclists in the era before female emancipation, and an unintentionally humorous section instructing young gentlemen how to make their cycle and then ride it.

A Victorian Cyclist features over 200 illustrations, and is complemented by a fully updated website.

"Lovely...wonderfully written...terrific" (Everything Bicycles)

"Rare and insightful" (Kent on Sunday)

"Interesting...informative...detailed historical insights" (BikeBiz)

"Unique and fascinating book...quality is very good...of considerable interest" (Veteran-Cycle Club)

"Superb...illuminating...well detailed...The easy flowing prose, which has a cadence like cycling itself, carries the reader along as if freewheeling with a hind wind" (Forty Plus Cycling Club)

"a fascinating book with both vivid descriptions and a number of hitherto-unseen photos of the area" ('Pedalling Pensioner', amazon.co.uk)

ISBN: 978-0-9559219-7-1

Also available on Kindle

Bicycle Beginnings
The Advent of the Bicycle or Velocipede... and what people of the 19th century were really saying about it
Stephen Channing

Cycling is such a natural activity for millions of people around the globe now, it is difficult to imagine that a little over a century ago many regarded it as reprehensible, revolting, or indeed revolutionary. The best way to get a feel for what early 'velocipedists' encountered is to read the words of the times, and this book gathers into one volume the most enlightening, entertaining and extraordinary insights from contemporary sources.

The mammoth work (over 190,000 words, covering the period 1779 to 1912) contains race reports, legal developments, technical innovations and inventions, records, advertisements, acrobatics, clothing, poems, arguments for and against the new-fangled vehicles, debates over women cyclists, and a long travelogue, "Berlin to Budapest on a Bicycle" capturing the excitement of a forgotten age of adventure on two wheels.

Not all the inventions were two-wheeled, however. This book also reveals the numerous variations that came into being before makers standardized on the shapes we commonly see nowadays: tricycles, ice velocipedes, water-paddle hobby-horses... These are explained with the aid of numerous illustrations, covering the gamut from cartoons to technical drawings and photographs. Even the race reports demonstrate far more variety than we are accustomed to seeing: 'ordinaries' (penny farthings) versus 'safety' bicycles versus tandems, monocycles, dwarf cycles, tricycles, double tricycles, four-wheel velocipedes, horses, ice skaters, steamships...

Rather than a single narrative to be read in one go, it is an anthology of fascinating glimpses into cycling's 'golden age', providing a new understanding of a bygone age of experimentation and much amusement, whenever the reader dips into it.

ISBN: 978-1-5210-8632-2
Also available on Kindle

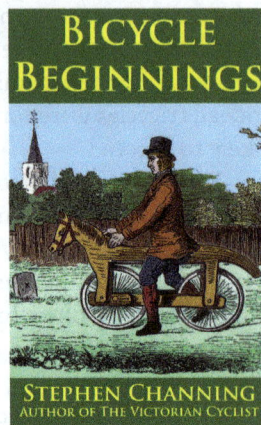

The Call of Cairnmor
Book One of the Cairnmor Trilogy
Sally Aviss

The Scottish Isle of Cairnmor is a place of great beauty and undisturbed wilderness, a haven for wildlife, a land of white sandy beaches and inland fertile plains, a land where awe-inspiring mountains connect precipitously with the sea.

To this remote island comes a stranger, Alexander Stewart, on a quest to solve the mysterious disappearance of two people and their unborn child; a missing family who are now heirs to a vast fortune. He enlists the help of local schoolteacher, Katherine MacDonald, and together they seek the answers to this enigma: a deeply personal journey that takes them from Cairnmor to the historic splendour of London and the industrial heartland of Glasgow.

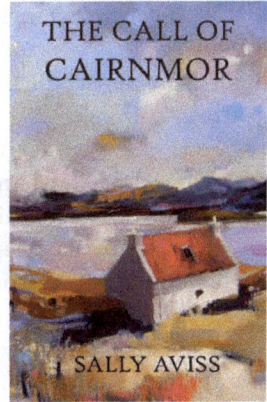

Covering the years 1936-1937 and infused with period colour and detail, The Call of Cairnmor is about unexpected discovery and profound attachment which, from its gentle opening, gradually gathers momentum and complexity until all the strands come together to give life-changing revelations.

"really enjoyed reading this – loved the plot...Read it in just two sittings as I couldn't stop reading." (P. Green – amazon.co.uk)

"exciting plot, not a book you want to put down, although I tried not to rush it so as to fully enjoy escaping to the world skilfully created by the author. A most enjoyable read." (Liz Green – amazon.co.uk)

"an excellent read. I cannot wait for the next part of the trilogy from this talented author. You will not want to put it down" (B. Burchell – amazon.co.uk)

ISBN: 978-0-9559219-9-5

Also available on Kindle

Changing Tides, Changing Times
Book Two of the Cairnmor Trilogy
Sally Aviss

In the dense jungle of Malaya in 1942, Doctor Rachel Curtis stumbles across a mysterious, unidentifiable stranger, badly injured and close to death.

Four years earlier in 1938 in London, Katherine Stewart and her husband Alex come into conflict with their differing needs while Alex's father, Alastair, knows he must keep his deeper feelings hidden from the woman he loves; a woman to whom he must never reveal the full extent of that love.

Covering a broad canvas and meticulously researched, Changing Times, Changing Tides follows the interwoven journey of well-loved characters from The Call of Cairnmor, as well as introducing new personalities, in a unique combination of novel and history that tells a story of love, loss, friendship and heroism; absorbing the reader in the characters' lives as they are shaped and changed by the ebb and flow of events before, during and after the Second World War.

"I enjoyed the twists and turns of this book…particularly liked the gutsy Dr Rachel who is a reminder to the reader that these are dark days for the world. Love triumphs but not in the way we thought it would and our heroine, Katherine, learns that the path to true love is certainly not a smooth one." (MDW – amazon.co.uk)

"Even better than the first book! A moving and touching story well told." (P. Green – amazon.co.uk)

"One of the best reads this year…can't wait for the next one." (Mr C. Brownett – amazon.co.uk)

"One of my favourite books – and I have shelves of them in the house! Sally Aviss is a masterful storyteller [...She] has obviously done a tremendous amount of research, judging by all the fascinating and in-depth historical detail woven into the storyline." ('Inverneill' – amazon.co.uk)

ISBN: 978-0-9931587-0-4

Also available on Kindle

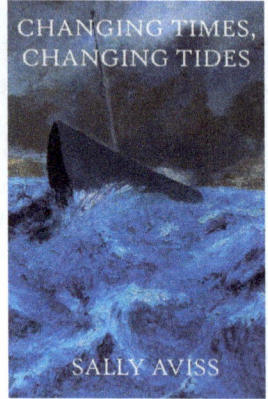

Where Gloom and Brightness Meet
Book Three of the Cairnmor Trilogy
Sally Aviss

When Anna Stewart begins a relationship with journalist Marcus Kendrick, the ramifications are felt from New York all the way across the Atlantic to the remote and beautiful Scottish island of Cairnmor, where her family live. Yet even as she and Marcus draw closer, Anna cannot forget her estranged husband whom she has not seen for many years.

When tragedy strikes, for some, Cairnmor becomes a refuge, a place of solace to ease the troubled spirit and an escape from painful reality; for others, it becomes a place of enterprise and adventure – a place in which to dream of an unfettered future.

This third book in the *Cairnmor Trilogy*, takes the action forward into the late nineteen-sixties as well as recalling familiar characters' lives from the intervening years. *Where Gloom and Brightness Meet* is a story of heartbreak and redemptive love; of long-dead passion remembered and retained in isolation; of unfaltering loyalty and steadfast devotion. It is a story that juxtaposes the old and the new; a story that reflects the conflicting attitudes, problems and joys of a liberating era.

"the last book in Sally Aviss's trilogy and it did not disappoint…what a wonderful journey this has been…cleverly written with an enormous amount of research" (B. Burchell – amazon.co.uk)

"I loved this third book in the series…the characters were believable and events unfolded in a beguiling way…not too happy ending for everyone but a satisfying conclusion to the saga" (P. Green – amazon.co.uk)

ISBN: 978-0-9931587-1-1

Also available on Kindle

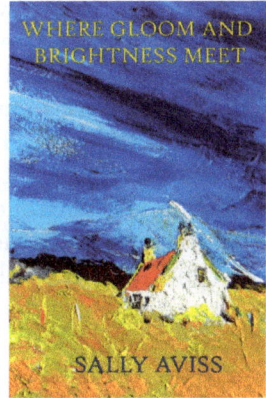

Message from Captivity
Sally Aviss

When diplomat's daughter Sophie Langley is sent on an errand of mercy to the Channel Island of St Nicolas in order to care for her two elderly aunts, she finds herself trapped in an unenviable position following the German invasion.

In the Battle for France, linguist and poet Robert Anderson, a lieutenant in the Royal Welch Fusiliers, finds himself embroiled in an impossible military situation from which there seems to be no escape.

From the beautiful Channel Islands to the very heart of Nazi-occupied Europe, Message From Captivity weaves factual authenticity into the fabric of a narrative where the twists and turns of captivity, freedom and dangerous pursuit have unforeseen consequences; where Robert's integrity is tested to the limit and Sophie needs all her inner strength to cope with the decisions and challenges she faces.

"The structure of the book takes you between the main protagonists and weaves their lives together as the story unfolds, add to that authentic research on the events of the period and you have a great story which keeps you guessing to the end." (P. Green – amazon.co.uk)

ISBN: 978-0-9931587-5-9

Also available on Kindle

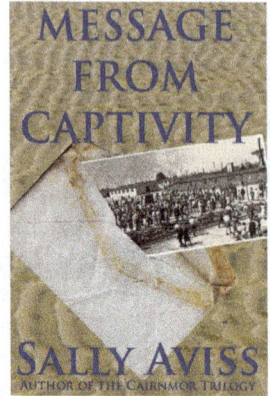

The Girl in Jack's Portrait

Sally Aviss

When struggling barrister Callie Martin encounters soldier Jamie Rutherford on ceremonial duty near Horse Guards Parade, her life is changed forever. When Edie Paignton's ex-husband deprives her of alimony, she puts her lovingly restored Victorian house up for sale and finds her life transformed by a chance meeting with architect Ben Rutherford, Jamie's father. When successful businessman Erik van der Waals discovers an unknown name and telephone number on a piece of paper, he determines to meet the owner. And when mental health nurse, Sarah Adhabi, embarks on a dangerous new relationship, she discovers she is more than a match for the new man in her life.

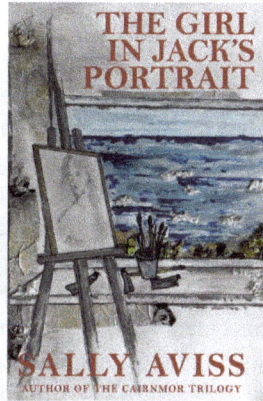

Six people seeking an escape from their pasts; six people seeking redemption in the present; six people who find their lives interwoven and their secrets revealed.

But just who is the Girl in Jack's Portrait?

ISBN: 978-0-9931587-6-6
Also available on Kindle

Ichigensan
– The Newcomer –
David Zoppetti
Translated from the Japanese by Takuma Sminkey

Ichigensan is a novel which can be enjoyed on many levels – as a delicate, sensual love story, as a depiction of the refined society in Japan's cultural capital Kyoto, and as an exploration of the themes of alienation and prejudice common to many environments, regardless of the boundaries of time and place.

Unusually, it shows Japan from the eyes of both an outsider and an 'internal' outcast, and even more unusually, it originally achieved this through sensuous prose carefully crafted by a non-native speaker of Japanese. The fact that this best-selling novella then won the Subaru Prize, one of Japan's top literary awards, and was also nominated for the Akutagawa Prize is a testament to its unique narrative power.

The story is by no means chained to Japan, however, and this new translation by Takuma Sminkey will allow readers world-wide to enjoy the multitude of sensations engendered by life and love in an alien culture.

"*A beautiful love story*" (*Japan Times*)

"*Sophisticated...subtle...sensuous...delicate...memorable...vivid depictions*" (*Asahi Evening News*)

"*Striking...fascinating...*" (*Japan PEN Club*)

"*Refined and sensual*" (*Kyoto Shimbun*)

"*quiet, yet very compelling...subtle mixture of humour and sensuality...the insights that the novel gives about Japanese society are both intriguing and exotic*" (*Nicholas Greenman, amazon.com*)

ISBN: 978-0-9559219-4-0

Also available on Kindle

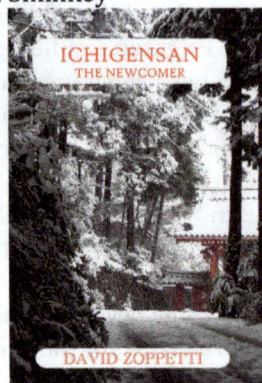

Sunflowers
– Le Soleil –
Shimako Murai
A play in one act
Translated from the Japanese by Ben Jones

Hiroshima is synonymous with the first hostile use of an atomic bomb. Many people think of this occurrence as one terrible event in the past, which is studied from history books.

Shimako Murai and other 'Women of Hiroshima' believe otherwise: for them, the bomb had after-effects which affected countless people for decades, effects that were all the more menacing for their unpredictability – and often, invisibility.

This is a tale of two such people: on the surface successful modern women, yet each bearing underneath hidden scars as horrific as the keloids that disfigured Hibakusha on the days following the bomb.

"a great story and a glimpse into the lives of the people who lived during the time of the war and how the bomb affected their lives, even after all these years" (Wendy Pierce, goodreads.com)

ISBN: 978-0-9559219-3-3

Also available on Kindle and Google Books

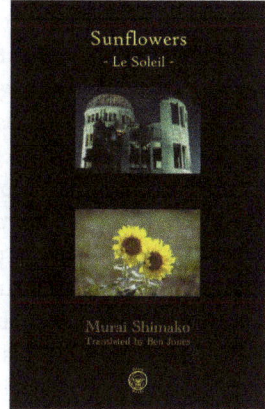

The Body as a Vessel
Approaching the Methodology of
Hijikata Tatsumi's Ankoku Butō
Mikami Kayo
An analysis of the modern dance form
Translated from the Japanese by Rosa van Hensbergen

When Hijikata Tatsumi's "Butō" appeared in 1959, it revolutionized not only Japanese dance but also the concept of performance art worldwide. It has however proved notoriously difficult to define or tie down. Mikami was a disciple of Hijikata for three years, and in this book, partly based on her graduate and doctoral theses, she combines insights from these years with earlier notes from other dancers to decode the ideas and processes behind butō.

ISBN: 978-0-9931587-4-2

Courtly Feasts to Kremlin Banquets
A History of Celebration and Hospitality:
Echoes of Russia's cuisine
Mikami Oksana Zakharova and Sergey Pushkaryov
Translated & adapted by Marina George

This is a book not only for lovers of food but also for those with an appetite for adventure and a thirst for the discovery of exciting gastronomic delights.

Russian history presents us with a rich tapestry of extravagant ceremony, characterized not only by the magnificent grandeur of individual courtly feasts but also by successive generations of nobility actively vying with each other to surpass the splendour created by their predecessors. Russian hospitality has always exuded a special vitality and sense of warm-hearted sociability. In Old Russia there was also a significant link between hospitality and the teachings of the Orthodox Church.

The political and social history of Russia has seen some very violent changes. The more shocking the political events of a country, the more brutal the cultural changes can be. At times, the differences between the past and the present are so extreme that one is faced with completely different worlds. Despite dramatic and often heart-breaking upheavals, we do surely have a duty to remember those distant roots that helped to nourish the present.

"Modern society contemptuously dismisses and sneers at the former way of life and deliberately breaks any connection with the past, which would always have been held to be so dear at the time." These words of writer, historian and theatre critic Yevgeny Opochinint were published in 1909 before the full horror of the revolutionary upheaval. The relevance of such remarks is surely as valid now as then.

Throughout history, special events have been an important way of imparting tradition from one generation to another, and symbolic meanings can still be found, if one knows the stories from the past. One just has to know where to look.

So, it is time to raise a toast in memory of bygone custom and tradition and to celebrate that great warm-hearted generosity of the Russian people.

ISBN: 978-0-9931587-8-0

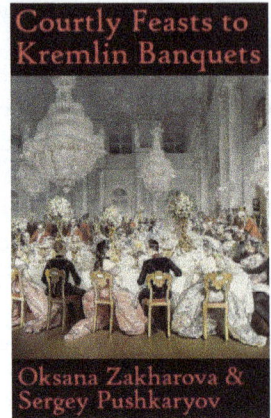

Misadventures at Margate – A Legend of Jarvis's Jetty
Thomas Ingoldsby
illustrated by Ernest Jessop

This lavishly illustrated facsimile edition comprises a humorous story about the adventures of a 19th century London gentleman visiting the seaside resort of Margate. There he naively befriends a poor 'vulgar boy', only to have his trust betrayed... A quaint fable from the Victorian era, or a cautionary tale for modern-day DFLs coming 'down from London' to explore Thanet's nooks and crannies (and crooks and nannies)? Some of the faces depicted in Jessop's wonderful cartoons can still be found in the side streets around Margate Pier and the Turner Contemporary art gallery! The verse – in rhyming couplets throughout – forms part of the ever popular Ingoldsby Legends. An appendix also explains the witty references that pepper the poem, and some terms that may be unfamiliar to modern readers.

ISBN: 978-0-9931587-9-7

Curling Wisps & Whispers of History
LucyAnn Curling
Vol. 1: Thanet to Tasmania

If family history is about gathering as many ancestors as possible, this book fails: it focuses on just three generations of the author's paternal side, between 1780 and 1826. At first nothing stirs the still waters of centuries of East Kent farming tradition. Men organize parish affairs, women follow domestic routines, boys attend a boarding school in Ramsgate, and only grandma seems interested in socializing or travel. Why then did Thomas Oakley Curling uproot everything and take his family on a marathon five-month voyage to Van Diemen's Land? Why leave one child behind? And where does Sir Charles Napier fit in?

Curling Wisps & Whispers of History
Vol. 1: Thanet to Tasmania

LucyAnn Curling

The genealogical quest starts naturally with a family heirloom, but soon tangential questions emerge, as multiple threads are collated and woven into one story. 'Georgian & Regency ancestors' might sound remote, removed from our reality, but the individuals' letters draw us into their world, and copious illustrations punctuate the text, animating the environments in which they lived.

"a superbly-produced family history [...] well-illustrated, and with no less than one hundred pages of appendices [...] this is an essential read for anyone [...] who has an interest in life in Kent in the 18th and 19th centuries." (Kent Family History Society)

ISBN 978-1-915174-02-4

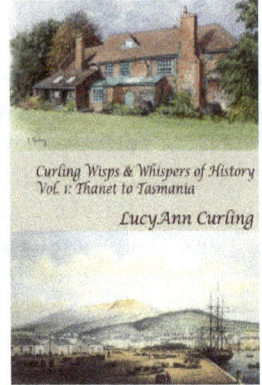

Vol. 2: Kent to Kefalonia

This second volume finds the Curling family back in England, struggling to find a financial foothold in society. Second son, Edward, has an unrewarding job in an attorney's office when Charles James Napier offers him a golden opportunity on the island of Kefalonia.

Follow the surprising twists of providence as Edward works on Napier's unusual project. What is the Malta connection? Tensions between Napier and his line manager, Sir Frederick Adam, have repercussions for Edward. Greece at this time was fighting for independence from the Ottoman Empire, and that war touches Napier's personal life obliquely but with lasting effect, while Edward's too is permanently changed by a

Curling Wisps & Whispers of History
Vol. 2: Kent to Kefalonia

LucyAnn Curling

different encounter. Edward's work journal and numerous letters in the Napier Papers at the British and Bodleian Libraries bear witness to the social pressures acting on all members of this extended clan, as their feelings come into conflict with accepted norms, and set the stage for further dramatic developments...

ISBN 978-1-915174-07-9

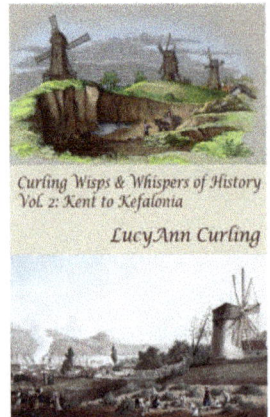

Watch and Ward
A History of Margate Borough Police 1858 to 1943
Nigel Cruttenden

A comprehensive history of Margate Borough Police from its inception in 1858 until its amalgamation into Kent County Constabulary in 1943. It covers the origins of the modern police force, detailing the influence of local councillors, JPs, solicitors and freemasons, as well as central government and world events such as the Boer War and two subsequent world wars.

Alongside its new prosperity, the up-and-coming Victorian seaside resort also had an underbelly watched over by the boys in blue. The borough's residents and visitors encountered issues similar to those of today, ranging from nuisance dogs and speeding vehicles through to mental health, alcohol abuse, domestic violence and assault – even the occasional murder. This book therefore also serves as a social history of East Kent, offering local, social and police historians copious material for research. Whenever an incident occurred in Margate, a policeman would be lurking nearby: a police man, indeed, as there were no warranted female police officers until after amalgamation. Women did however also play an important role within Margate Police, as the book shows.

This is also an invaluable reference work for genealogists or other enthusiasts researching family history in and around Thanet. Family Trees are all very well, but they do not put the flesh on the bones, and even internet searches are quite limited. Full indices make it easy for modern Margatonians and Thanetians to check whether their ancestors might have been 'involved' with the police – on whichever side!

"without a doubt this book raises the bar ... a well-researched and comprehensive account ... serious students ... will not be disappointed" (Police History Society)

ISBN 978-1-915174-03-1

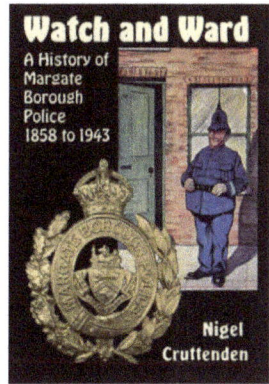